THE
BIBLE
In Word and Art

sophisticated, it started to change dramatically from the 16th century onward, when illustrations became more scenic, detailed, and decorative. A predecessor of Matthäus Merian's illustrated Bible must also be seen in the graphic Bible cycles, which mostly dealt with the passion story of Jesus – such as the engravings of Schongauer or Cranach the Elder and the Dürer cycles.

During the reformation, the spread of the Bible and its sections, especially Luther's translation, increased rapidly. In Augsburg alone, more than 100 illustrated Bibles were published by 1626.

Luther, himself, planned the publication of an illustrated Protestant Bible – the "Leyenbibel" – the Bible for the layman. His Bible for the layman was to be a biblical picture book for children and less-educated people with the intention of facilitating memorization of the biblical stories.

Another Bible, published in 1534, was the Luffts Vollbibel, a complete Bible in which Luther determined the illustrations and their allocation in the text. The first edition of the Bible was illustrated with 117 woodcuts.

Neither Lutherans nor reformed Protestants extended a latent iconoclastic attitude towards Bible illustrations.

They agreed that like it or not, the word Christianity ellicited the vision of a man nailed to the cross. Because it was not a sin to have his image in their heart, why should it have been a sin if their eyes beheld it?

In the early 17th century, engravings began to supersede the woodcuts formerly inserted between the text. One such illustrated Bible contains the engravings by Matthäus Merian, and has since become almost proverbially known as the "Merian-Bible."

THE MERIAN ILLUSTRATIONS

The Merian engravings from copper plates were first published in Strasburg in 1625, and again two years later in Frankfurt under the title "Biblische Abbildungen zur Darstellung der wichtigsten Geschichten der heiligen Schrift," Icones Biblicae, as a collection of Bible illustrations entitled "Die wichtigsten Ereignisse und Visionen des Neuen Testaments" (The Most Important Events and Visions of the New Testament).

In 1628, a publishing house in Amsterdam issued a collection of biblical illustrations with English, French, and German text, for which Merian produced 258 engravings. In 1630, the printer and publisher Lazarus Zetzner printed a German Bible, which was to become the Merian-Bible, containing the latest edition of Martin Luther's translation and 233 engravings by Matthäus Merian.

Compared with the already established canon of Bible illustrations based on Luther's own specifications, Merian now successfully introduced a totally different, independent personal interpretation.

For his new series of illustrations Merian chose highly dramatic scenes which illuminate crucial situations of life: birth, initiation, consecration, ritual, retreat and sacrifice, conflict, despair and struggle, lust, temptation, love and pain, searching and finding, blasphemy and pardon, the search for God, trial and en-

lightment, magic, prophecy and transfiguration, destruction and deliverance, disease, penury and restoration, fall and recovery, death and the devil, judgment, fall and salvation, and so on. The baroque scenery of his engravings had penetrating depth and a frequently amazing wealth of detail, which has a certain qualifying effect and takes some weight off the dramatic events thus guiding the beholder to a different focus. For instance, in Jacob's house, a tame bird perched on a pole turns its back on events; a dog paces around the golden calf apparently expecting miracles from it. In another illustration a man in the background continues to row his boat to the shore while Gideon in the foreground receives a message from an angel. Or a man and a woman walk quietly conversing through the forest while Samson is about to kill a lion with his hands. And in Martha's house, fowl is happily being plucked in the foreground as Jesus explains his message of salvation to Martha's sister Mary.

Consequently, Merian's illustrations have come a long way from Luther's request to depict the contents of the text without any superfluous detail. Instead, Merian appears to have tried to open new avenues toward the understanding of the Holy Scriptures to the reader.

During his first stay in Frankfurt Matthäus Merian met the Rosenkreutzer, a secret society named after the legendary Christian Rosenkreuz, and Michael Maier.

In 1619, with the help of Matthäus Merian, Maier published his work, The Fugitive Atlanta, which contained new alchimistic emblems of the secrets of nature. This volume is an occult book which is generally acknowledged to be the most beautiful, if not the most curious, work of the esoteric alchemy of the 17th century.

It contains fifty emblems magnificently engraved by Merian, each emblem in turn consisting of a fantastic allegorical picture, a proverb, and an epigram. It was this collaboration with Maier that gave Merian a different understanding of the Holy Scriptures.

Thus, the Christian religion was an ancient occult doctrine confirmed by the Bible as well as by nature. The two testaments and nature were interrelated, with all three combining to form a concordance. Therefore, the Bible could be used and interpreted in the cabbalistic sense by the initiated.

Merian, himself, specifies his intention as "being able to differently impress the mind of the beholder by an impressioned contemplation of his pictures." Above all he felt that the special execution of his engravings was suitable to counteract such strong appeals as were protrayed in paintings as the "Frivolus Venus" or "Petri's Infamous Pranks," which he considered vexing inventions. He also hoped to achieve a deeper impression on a different mental and emotional level.

THE COLORING
OF THE MERIAN-BIBLE

he additional coloring of Matthäus Merian's engravings in a copy of the Strasburg edition of 1630 probably dates back to the 17th century. It was executed in a rather elaborate and costly way with opaque

The Art of
the Old Testament

n the beginning God created the heaven and the earth. ²And the earth was without form, and void; and darkness was upon the face of the deep. And the spirit of God moved upon the face of the waters. ³And God said, Let there be light: and there was light. ⁴And God saw the light, that it was good: and God divided the light from the darkness. ⁵And God called the light Day, and the darkness he called Night. And the evening and the morning were the first day. ⁶And God said, let there be a firmament in the midst of the waters, and let it divide the waters from the waters. ⁷And God made the firmament, and divided the waters which were under the firmament from the waters which were above the firmament: and it was so. ⁸And God called the firmament heaven. And the evening and the morning were the second day. ⁹And God said, Let the waters under the heaven be gathered together unto one place, and let the dry land appear: and it was so. ¹⁰And God called the dry land earth: and the gathering together of the waters called he seas: and God saw that it was good. ¹¹And God said, Let the earth bring forth grass, the herb yielding seed, and the fruit tree yielding fruit after his kind, whose seed is in itself, upon the earth: and it was so. ¹²And the earth brought forth grass, and herb yielding seed after his kind, and the tree yielding fruit, whose seed was in itself, after his kind: and God saw that it was good. ¹³And the evening and the morning were the third day. ¹⁴And God said, let there be lights in the firmament of the heaven to divide the day from the night; and let them be for signs, and for seasons, and for days, and years: ¹⁵And let them be for lights in the firmament of the heaven to give light upon the earth: and it was so. ¹⁶And God made two great lights; the greater light to rule the day, and the lesser light to rule the night: he made the stars also. ¹⁷And God set them in the firmament of the heaven to give light upon the earth, ¹⁸and to rule over the day and over the night, and to divide the light from the darkness: and God saw that it was good. ¹⁹And the evening and the morning were the fourth day. ²⁰And God said, Let the waters bring forth abundantly the moving creature

that hath life, and fowl that may fly above the earth in the open firmament of heaven. ²¹And God created great whales, and every living creature that moveth, which the waters brought forth abundantly, after their kind, and every winged fowl after his kind: and God

saw that it was good. [22]And God blessed them, saying, be fruitful, and multiply, and fill the waters in the seas, and let fowl multiply in the earth. [23]And the evening and the morning were the fifth day. [24]And God said, Let the earth bring forth the living creature after his kind, cattle, and creeping thing, and beast of the earth after his kind: and it was so. [25]And God made the beast of the earth after his kind, and cattle after their kind, and every thing that creepeth upon the earth after his kind: and God saw that it was good.

nd God said, Let us make man in our image, after our likeness: and let them have dominion over the fish of the sea, and over the fowl of the air, and over the cattle, and over all the earth, and over every creeping thing that creepeth upon the earth. [27]So God created man in his own image, in the image of God created he him; male and female created he them. [28]And God blessed them, and God said unto them, Be fruitful, and multiply, and replenish the earth, and subdue it: and have dominion over the fish of the sea, and over the fowl of the air, and over every living thing that moveth upon the earth. [29]And God said, Behold, I have given you every herb bearing seed, which is upon the face of all the earth, and every tree, in the which is the fruit of a tree yielding seed; to you it shall be for meat. [30]And to every beast of the earth, and to every fowl of the air, and to every thing that creepeth upon the earth, wherein there is life, I have given every green herb for meat: and it was so. [31]And God saw every thing that he had made, and, behold, it was very good. And the evening and the morning were the sixth day.

ow the serpent was more subtil than any beast of the field which the LORD God had made. And he said unto the woman, Yea, hath God said, Ye shall not eat of every tree of the garden? [2]And the woman said unto the serpent, We may eat of the fruit of the trees of the garden: [3]But of the fruit of the tree which is in the midst of the garden, God hath said, Ye shall not eat of it, neither shall ye touch it, lest ye die. [4]And the serpent said unto the woman, Ye shall not surely die: [5]For God doth know that in the day ye eat thereof, then your eyes shall be opened, and ye shall be as gods, knowing good and evil. [6]And when the woman saw that the tree was good for food, and that it was pleasant to the eyes, and a tree to be desired to make one wise, she took of the fruit thereof, and did eat, and gave also unto her husband with her; and he did eat. [7]And the eyes of them both were opened, and they knew that they were naked; and they sewed fig leaves together, and made themselves aprons.

nd the LORD God said unto the serpent, Because thou hast done this, thou art cursed above all cattle, and above every beast of the field; upon thy belly shalt thou go, and dust shalt thou eat all the days of thy life: [15]And I will put enmity between me and the woman, and between thy seed and her seed; it shall bruise thy head, and thou shalt bruise his heel. [16]Unto the woman he said, I will greatly multiply thy sorrow and thy coneption; in sorrow thou shalt bring forth children; and thy desire shall be to thy husband, and he shall rule over thee. [17]And unto Adam he said, Because thou hast hearkened unto the voice of thy wife, and hast eaten of the tree, of which I commanded thee, saying, thou shalt not eat of it all the days of thy life; [18]Thorns also and thistles shall it bring forth to thee; and thou shalt eat the herb of the field; [19]In the sweat of thy face shalt thou eat bread, till thou return unto the ground; for out of it wast thou taken: for dust thou art, and unto dust shalt thou return. [20]And Adam called his wife's name Eve; because she was the mother of all living.

nto Adam also and to his wife did the LORD God make coats of skins, and clothed them. [22]And the LORD God said, Behold, the man is become as one of us, to know good and evil: and now, lest he put forth his hand, and take also of the tree of life, and eat, and live for ever: [23]Therefore the LORD God sent him forth from the garden of Eden, to till the ground from whence he was taken. [24]So he drove out the man; and he placed at the east of the garden of Eden Cher-u-bims, and a flaming sword which turned every way, to keep the way of the tree of life.

nd Adam knew Eve his wife; and she conceived, and bare Cain, and said, I have gotten a man from the LORD. ²And she again bare his brother Abel. And Abel was a keeper of sheep, but Cain was a tiller of the ground. ³And in process of time it came to pass, that Cain brought of the fruit of the ground an offering unto the LORD. ⁴And Abel, he also brought of the firstlings of his flock and of the fat thereof. And the LORD had respect unto Abel and to his offering: ⁵But unto Cain and to his offering he had not respect. And Cain was very wroth, and his countenance fell. ⁶And the LORD said unto Cain, Why art thou wroth? and why is thy countenance fallen? ⁷If thou doest well, shalt thou not be accepted? and if thou doest not well, sin lieth at the door. And unto thee shall be his desire, and thou shalt rule over him. ⁸And Cain talked with Abel his brother: and it came to pass, when they were in the field, that Cain rose up against Abel his brother, and slew him. ⁹And the LORD said unto Cain, where is Abel thy brother? And he said, I know not: Am I my brother's keeper? ¹⁰And he said, what hast thou done? The voice of thy brother's blood crieth unto me from the ground. ¹¹And now art thou cursed from the earth, which hath opened her mouth to receive thy brother's blood from thy hand; ¹²When thou tillest the ground, it shall not henceforth yield unto thee her strength; a fugitive and an vagabond shalt thou be in the earth.

hese are the generations of Noah: Noah was a just man and perfect in his generations, and Noah walked with God. [10]And Noah begat three sons, Shem, Ham, and Ja-pheth. [11]The earth also was corrupt before God, and the earth was filled with violence. [12]And God looked upon the earth, and, behold, it was corrupt; for all flesh had corrupted his way upon the earth. [13]And God said unto Noah, the end of all flesh is come before me; for the earth is filled with violence through them; and, behold, I will destroy them with the earth. [14]Make thee an ark of gopher wood; rooms shalt thou make in the ark, and shalt pitch it within and without with pitch. [15]And this is the fashion which thou shalt make it of: The length of the ark shall be three hundred cubits, the breadth of it fifty cubits, and the height of it thirty cubits. [16]A window shalt thou make to the ark, and in a cubit shalt thou finish it above; and the door of the ark shalt thou set in the side thereof; with lower, second, and third stories shalt thou make it. [17]And, behold, I, even I, do bring a flood of waters upon the earth, to destroy all flesh, wherein is the breath of life, from under heaven; and every thing that is in the earth shall die. [18]But with thee will I establish my covenant; and thou shalt come into the ark, thou, and thy sons, and thy wife, and thy sons' wives with thee. [19]And of every living thing of all flesh, two of every sort shalt thou bring into the ark, to keep them alive with thee; they shall be male and female. [20]Of fowls after their kind, and of cattle after their kind, of every creeping thing of the earth after his kind, two of every sort shall come unto thee, to keep them alive. [21]And take thou unto thee of all food that is eaten, and thou shalt gather it to thee; and it shall be for food for thee, and for them. [22]Thus did Noah; according to all that God commanded him, so did he.

nd the flood was forty days upon the earth; and the waters increased, and bare up the ark, and it was lifted up above the earth. [18]And the waters prevailed exceedingly upon the earth; and all the high hills, that were under the whole heaven, were covered. [20]Fifteen cubits upward did the waters prevail; and the mountains were covered. [21]And all flesh died that moved upon the earth, both of fowl, and of cattle, and of beast, and of every creeping thing that creepeth upon the earth, and every man: [22]All in whose nostrils was the breath of life, of all that was in the dry land, died. [23]And every living substance was destroyed which was upon the face of the ground, both man, and cattle, and the creeping things, and the fowl of the heaven; and they were destroyed from the earth: and Noah only remained alive, and they that were with him in the ark. [24]And the waters prevailed upon the earth an hundred and fifty days.

nd God spake unto Noah, and to his sons with him, saying, [9]And I, behold, I establish my covenant with you, and with your seed after you; [10]And with every living creature that is with you, of the fowl, of the cattle, and of every beast of the earth with you; from all that go out of the ark, to every beast of the earth. [11]And I will establish my covenant with you; neither shall all flesh be cut off any more by the waters of a flood; neither shall there any more be a flood to destroy the earth. [12]And God said, This is the token of the covenant which I make between me and you and every living creature that is with you, for perpetual generations: [13]I do set my bow in the cloud, and it shall be for a token of a covenant between me and the earth. [14]And it shall come to pass, when I bring a cloud over the earth, that the bow shall be seen in the cloud: [15]And I will remember my covenant, which is between me and you and every living creature of all flesh; and the waters shall no more become a flood to destroy all flesh. [16]And the bow shall be in the cloud; and I will look upon it, that I may remember the everlasting covenant between God and every living creature of all flesh that is upon the earth. [17]And God said unto Noah, This is the token of the covenant, which I have established between me and all flesh that is upon the earth.

nd the sons of Noah, that went forth of the ark, were Shem, and Ham, and Japheth: and Ham is the father of Canaan. ¹⁹These are the three sons of Noah: and of them was the whole earth overspread. ²⁰And Noah began to be an husbandman, and he planted a vineyard: ²¹And he drank of the wine, and was drunken; and he was uncovered within his tent. ²²And Ham, the father of Canaan, saw the nakedness of his father, and told his two brethren without. ²³And Shem and Japheth took a garment, and laid it upon both their shoulders, and went backward, and covered the nakedness of their father; and their faces were backward, and they saw not their father's nakedness. ²⁴And Noah awoke from his wine, and knew what his younger son had done unto him. ²⁵And he said, Cursed be Canaan; a servant of servants shall he be unto his brethren. ²⁶And he said, Blessed be the

Lord God of Shem; and Canaan shall be his servant. ²⁷God shall enlarge Japheth, and he shall dwell in the tents of Shem; and Canaan shall be his servant. ²⁸And Noah lived after the flood three hundred and fifty years. ²⁹And all the days of Noah were nine hundred and fifty years; and he died.

nd whole earth was of one language, and of one speech. ²And it came to pass, as they journeyed from the east, that they found a plain in the land of Shinar; and they dwelt there. ³And they said one to another, Go to, let us make brick, and burn them throughly. And they had brick for stone, and slime had they for mortar. ⁴And they said, Go to, let us build us a city and a tower, whose top may reach unto heaven; and let us make us a name, lest we be scattered abroad upon the face of the whole earth. ⁵And the LORD came down to see the city and the tower, which the children of men builded. ⁶And the LORD said, Behold, the people is one, and they have all one language; and this they begin to do: and now nothing will be restrained from them, which they have imagined to do. ⁷Go to, let us go down, and there confound their language, that they may not understand one another's speech. ⁸So the LORD scattered them abroad from thence upon the face of all the earth: and they left off to build the city. ⁹Therefore is the name of it called Babel; because the LORD did there confound the language of all the earth: and from thence did the LORD scatter them abroad upon the face of all the earth.

ow the LORD had said unto Abram, Get thee out of thy country, and from thy kindred, and from thy father's house, unto a land that I will shew thee: ²And I will make of thee a great nation, and I will bless thee, and make thy name great; and thou shalt be a blessing: ³And I will bless them that bless thee, and curse him that curseth thee: and in thee shall all families of the earth be blessed. ⁴So Abram departed, as the LORD had spoken unto him; and Lot went with him: and Abram was seventy and five years old when he departed out of Haran. ⁵And Abram took Sarai his wife, and Lot his brother's son, and all their substance that they had gathered, and the souls that they had gotten in Haran; and they went forth to go into the land of Canaan; and into the land of Canaan they came. ⁶And Abram passed through the land unto the place of Sichem, unto the plain of Moreh. And the Canaanite was then in the land. ⁷And the LORD appeared unto Abram, and said, Unto thy seed will I give his land: and there builded he an altar unto the LORD, who appeared unto him. ⁸And he removed from thence unto a mountain on the east of Beth-el, and pitched his tent, having Beth-el on the west, and Hai on the east: and there he builded an altar unto the LORD, and called upon the name of the LORD. ⁹And Abram journeyed, going on still toward the south.

nd the king of Sodom went out to meet him after his return from the slaughter of Chedorlaomer, and of the kings that were with him, at the valley of Shaveh, which is the king's dale. [18]And Melchizedek king of Salem brought forth bread and wine: and he was the priest of the most high God. [19]And he blessed him, and said, Blessed be Abram of the most high God, possessor of heaven and earth: [20]And blessed be the most high God, which hath delivered thine enemies into thy hand. And he gave him tithes of all. [21]And the king of Sodom said unto Abram, Give me the persons, and take the goods to thyself. [22]And Abram said to the king of Sodom, I have lift up mine hand unto the Lord, the most high God, the possessor of heaven and earth, [23]That I will not take from a thread even to a shoelatchet, and that I will not take any thing that is thine, lest you shouldest say, I have made Abram rich: [24]Save only that which the young men have eaten, and the portion of the men which went with me, Aner, Eshcol, and Mamre; let them take their portion.

And the LORD appeared unto him in the plains of Mamre: and he sat in the tent door in the heat of the day; [2]And he lift up his eyes and looked, and, lo, three men stood by him: and when he saw them, he ran to meet them from the tent door, and bowed himself toward the ground, [3]And said, My LORD, if now I have found favor in thy sight, pass not away, I pray thee, from thy servant: [4]Let a little water, I pray you, be fetched, and wash your feet, and rest yourselves under the tree: [5]And I will fetch a morsel of bread, and comfort ye your hearts; after that ye shall pass on: for therefore are ye come to your servant. And they said, So do, as thou hast said. [6]And Abraham hastened into the tent unto Sarah, and said, Make ready quickly three measures of fine meal, knead it, and make cakes upon the hearth. [7]And Abraham ran unto the herd, and fetched a calf tender and good, and gave it unto a young man; and he hasted to dress it. [8]And he took butter, and milk, and the calf which he had dressed, and set it before them; and he stood by them under the tree, and they did eat.

And when the morning arose, then the angels hastened Lot, saying, Arise, take thy wife, and thy two daughters, which are here; lest thou be consumed in the inquity of the city. [16]And while he lingered, the men laid hold upon his hand, and upon the hand of his wife, and upon the hand of his two daughters; the LORD being merciful unto him; and they brought him forth, and set him without the city. [17]And it came to pass, when they had brought them forth abroad, that he said, Escape for thy life; look not behind thee, neither stay thou in all the plain; escape to the mountain, lest thou be consumed. [18]And Lot said unto them, Oh, not so, my LORD: [19]Behold now, thy servant hath found grace in thy sight, and thou hast shewed unto me in saving my life; and I cannot escape to the mountain, lest some evil take me, and I die: [20]Behold now, this city is near to flee unto, and it is a little one: Oh, let me escape thither, (is it not a little one?) and my soul shall live. [21]And he said unto him, See, I have accepted thee concerning this thing also, that I will not overthrow this city, for that which thou hast spoken. [22]Haste thee, escape thither; for I cannot do any thing till thou be come thither. Therefore the name of the city was called Zoar. [23]The sun was risen upon the earth when Lot entered into Zoar. [24]Then the LORD rained upon Sodom and upon Gomorrah brimstone and fire from the LORD out of heaven; [25]And he overthrew those cities, and all the plain, and all the inhabitants of the cities, and that which grew upon the ground. [26]But his wife looked back from behind him, and she became a pillar of salt.

nd Abraham rose up early in the morning, and took bread, and a bottle of water, and gave it unto Hagar, putting it on her shoulder, and the child, and sent her away: and she departed, and wandered in the wilderness of Beer-sheba. [15]And the water was spent in the bottle, and she cast the child under one of the shrubs. [16]And she went, and sat her down over against him a good way off, as it were a bowshot: for she said, Let me not see the death of the child. And she sat over against him, and lift up her voice, and wept. [17]And God heard the voice of the lad; and the angel of God called to Hagar out of heaven, and said unto her, What aileth thee, Hagar? fear not; for God hath heard the voice of the lad where he is. [18]Arise, lift up the lad, and hold him in thine hand; for I will make him a great nation. [19]And God opened her eyes, and she saw a well of water; and she went, and filled the bottle with water, and gave the lad drink. [20]And God was with the lad; and he grew, and dwelt in the wilderness, and became an archer. [21]And he dwelt in the wilderness of Paran: and his mother took him a wife out of the land of Egypt.

And Abraham rose up early in the morning, and saddled his ass, and took two of his young men with him, and Isaac his son, and clave the wood for the burnt offering, and rose up, and went unto the place of which God had told him. [4]Then on the third day Abraham lifted up his eyes, and saw the place afar off. [5]And Abraham said unto his young men, Abide ye here with the ass; and I and the lad will go yonder and worship, and come again to you. [6]And Abraham took the wood of the burnt offering, and laid it upon Isaac his son; and he took the fire in his hand, and a knife; and they went both of them together. [7]And Isaac spake unto Abraham his father, and said, My father: and he said, Here am I, my son. And he said, Behold the fire and the wood: but where is the lamb for a burnt offering? [8]And Abraham said, My son, God will provide himself a lamb for a burnt offer-ing: so they went both of them together. [9]And they came to the place which God had told him of; and Abraham built an altar there, and laid the wood in order, and bound Isaac his son, and laid him on the altar upon the wood. [10]And Abraham stretched forth his hand, and took the knife to slay his son. [11]And the angel of the Lord called unto him out of heaven, and said, Abraham, Abraham: and he said, Here am I. [12]And he said, Lay not thine hand upon the lad, neither do thou any thing unto him: for now I know that thou fearest God, seeing thou hast not witheld thy son, thine only son from me. [13]And Abraham lifted up his eyes, and looked, and behold behind him a ram caught in a thicket by his horns: and Abraham went and took the ram, and offered him up for a burnt offering in the stead of his son.

nd Isaac came from the way of the well Lahairoi; for he dwelt in the south country. [63]And Isaac went out to meditate in the field at the eventide: and he lifted up his eyes, and saw, and behold, the camels were coming. [64]And Rebekah lifted up her eyes, and when she saw Isaac, she lighted off the camel. [65]For she had said unto the servant, What man is this that walketh in the field to meet us? And the servant had said, It is my master: therefore she took a veil, and covered herself. [66]And the servant told Isaac all things that he had done. [67]And Isaac brought her into his mother Sarah's tent, and took Rebekah, and she became his wife; and he loved her: and Isaac was comforted after his mother's death.

nd these are the days of the years of Abraham's life which he lived, an hundred threescore and fifteen years. [8]Then Abraham gave up the ghost, and died in a good old age, an old man, and full of years; and was gathered to his people. [9]And his sons Isaac and Ishmael buried him in the cave of Machpelah, in the field of Ephron the son of Zohar the Hittite, which is before Mamre; [10]The field which Abraham purchased of the sons of Heth: there was Abraham buried, and Sarah his wife. [11]And it came to pass after the death of Abraham, that God blessed his son Isaac; and Isaac dwelt by the well Lahairoi.

nd the boys grew: and Esau was a cunning hunter, a man of the field; and Jacob was a plain man, dwelling in tents. ²⁸And Isaac loved Esau, because he did eat of his venison: but Rebekah loved Jacob. ²⁹And Jacob sod pottage: and Esau came from the field, and he was faint: ³⁰And Esau said to Jacob, Feed me, I pray thee, with that same red pottage; for I am faint: therefore was his name called Edom. ³¹And Jacob said, Behold, I am at the point to die; and what profit shall this birthright do to me? ³³And Jacob said, Swear to me this day; and he sware unto him; and he sold his birthright unto Jacob. ³⁴Then Jacob gave Esau bread and pottage of lentiles; and he did eat and drink, and rose up, and went his way; thus Esau despised his birthright.

nd he came unto his father, and said, My father; and he said, Here am I; who art thou, my son? ¹⁹And Jacob said unto his father, I am Esau thy firstborn; I have done according as thou badest me: arise, I pray thee, sit and eat my venison, that thy soul may bless me. ²⁰And Isaac said unto his son, How is it that you hast found it so quickly, my son? And he said, Because the LORD thy God brought it to me. ²¹And Isaac said unto Jacob, Come near, I pray thee, that I may feel thee, my son, whether thou be my very son Esau or not. ²²And Jacob went near unto Isaac his father; and felt him, and said, The voice is Jacob's voice, but the hands are the hands of Esau. ²³And he discerned him not, because his hands were hairy, as his brother Esau's hands: so he blessed him. ²⁴And he said, Art thou my very son Esau? And he said, I am. ²⁵And he said, Bring it near to me, and I will eat of my son's venison, that my soul may bless thee. And he brought it near to him, and he did eat: and he brought him wine, and he drank. ²⁶And his father Isaac said unto him, Come near now, and kiss me, my son. ²⁷And he came near, and kissed him: and he smelled the smell of his raiment, and blessed him, and said, See, the smell of my son is as the smell of a field which the LORD hath blessed: ²⁸Therefore God give thee of the dew of heaven, and the fatness of the earth, and plenty of corn and wine: ²⁹Let people serve thee, and nations bow down to thee: be lord over thy brethren, and let thy mother's sons bow down to thee: cursed be every one that curseth thee, and blessed be he that blesseth thee.

nd Jacob went out from Beer-sheba, and went toward Haran. ¹¹And he lighted upon a certain place, and tarried there all night, because the sun was set; and he took of the stones of that place, and put them for his pillows, and lay down in that place to sleep. ¹²And he dreamed, and behold a ladder set up on the earth, and the top of it reached to heaven: and behold the angels of God ascending and descending on it. ¹³And, behold, the LORD stood above it, and said, I am the LORD God of Abraham thy father, and the God of Isaac: the land whereon thou liest, to thee will I give it, and to thy seed; ¹⁴And thy seed shall be as the dust of the earth, and thou shalt spread abroad to the west, and to the east, and to the north, and to the south: and in thee and in thy seed shall all the families of the earth be blessed. ¹⁵And, behold, I am with thee, and will keep thee in all places whither thou goest, and will bring thee again into this land; for I will not leave thee, until I have done that which I have spoken to thee of. ¹⁶And Jacob awaked out of his sleep, and he said, Surely the LORD is in this place; and I knew it not. ¹⁷And he was afraid, and said, How dreadful is this place! this is none other but the house of God, and this is the gate of heaven. ¹⁸And Jacob rose up early in the morning, and took the stone that he had put for his pillows, and set it up for a pillar, and poured oil upon the top of it. ¹⁹And he called the name of that place Bethel: but the name of that city was called Luz at the first.

hen Jacob went on his journey, and came into the land of the people of the east. ²And he looked, and behold a well in the field, and, lo, there were three flocks of sheep lying by it; for out of that well they watered the flocks: and a great stone was upon the well's mouth. ³And thither were all the flocks gathered: and they rolled the stone from the well's mouth, and watered the sheep, and put the stone again upon the well's mouth in his place. ⁴And Jacob said unto them, My brethren, whence be ye? And they said, Of Haran are we. ⁵And he said unto them, Know ye Laban the son of Nahor? And they said, We know him. ⁶And he said unto them, Is he well? And they said, He is well: and, behold, Rachel his daughter cometh with the sheep. ⁷And he said, Lo, it is yet high day, neither is it time that the cattle should be gathered together: water ye the sheep, and go and feed them. ⁸And they said, We cannot, until all the flocks be gathered together, and till they roll the stone from the well's mouth; then we water the sheep. ⁹And while he yet spake with them, Rachel came with her father's sheep: for she kept them. ¹⁰And it came to pass, when Jacob saw Rachel the daughter of Laban his mother's brother, and the sheep of Laban his mother's brother, that Jacob went near, and rolled the stone from the well's mouth, and watered the flock of Laban his mother's brother.

nd he rose up that night, and took his two wives, and his two womenservants, and his eleven sons, and passed over the ford Jabbok. [23]And he took them, and sent them over the brook, and sent over that he had. [24]And Jacob was left alone; and there wrestled a man with him until the breaking of the day. [25]And when he saw that he prevailed not against him, he touched the hollow of his thigh; and the hollow of Jacob's thigh was out of joint, as he wrestled with him. [26]And he said, Let me go, for the day breaketh. And he said, I will not let thee go, except thou bless me. [27]And he said unto him, What is thy name? And he said, Jacob. [28]And he said, Thy name shall be called no more Jacob, but Israel: for as a prince hast thou power with God and with men, and hast prevailed. [29]And Jacob asked him, and said, Tell me, I pray thee, thy name. And he said, Wherefore is it that thou dost ask after my name? And he blessed him there. [30]And Jacob called the name of the place Peniel: for I have seen God face to face, and my life is preserved. [31]And as he passed over Penuel the sun rose upon him, and he halted upon his thigh. [32]Therefore the children of Israel eat not of the sinew which shrank, which is upon the hollow of the thigh, unto this day: because he touched the hollow of Jacob's thigh in the sinew that shrank.

 nd Jacob lifted up his eyes, and looked, and, behold, Esau came, and with him four hundred men. And he divided the children unto Leah, and unto Rachel, and unto the two handmaids. ²And he put the handmaids and their children foremost, and Leah and her children after, and Rachel and Joseph hindermost. ³And he passed over before them, and bowed himself to the ground seven times, until he came near to his brother. ⁴And Esau ran to meet him, and embraced him, and fell on his neck, and kissed him; and they wept. ⁵And he lifted up his eyes, and saw the women and the children; and said, Who are those with thee? And he said, The children which God hath graciously given thy servant. ⁶Then the handmaidens came near, they and their children, and they bowed themselves. ⁷And Leah also with her children came near, and bowed themselves: and after came Joseph near and Rachel, and they bowed themselves. ⁸And he said, What meanest thou by all this drove which I met? And he said, These are to find grace in the sight of my lord. ⁹And Esau said, I have enough, my brother; keep that thou hast unto thyself. ¹⁰And Jacob said, Nay, I pray thee, if now I have found grace in thy sight, then receive my present at my hand: for therefore I have seen thy face, as though I had seen the face of God, and thou wast pleased with me. ¹¹Take, I pray thee, my blessing that is brought to thee; because God hath dealt graciously with me, and because I have enough. And he urged him, and he took it.

And it came to pass on the third day, when they were sore, that two of the sons of Jacob, Simeon and Levi, Dinah's brethren, took each man his sword, and came upon the city boldly, and slew all the males. ²⁶And they slew Hamor and Shechem his son with the edge of the sword, and took Dinah out of Shechem's house, and went out. ²⁷The sons of Jacob came upon the slain, and spoiled the city, because they had defiled their sisters. ²⁸They took their sheep, and their oxen, and their asses, and that which was in the city, and that which was in the field, ²⁹And all their wealth, and all their little ones, and their wives took they captive, and spoiled even all that was in the house. ³⁰And Jacob said to Simeon and Levi, Ye have troubled me to make me to stink among the inhabitants of the land, among the Canaanites and the Perizzites: and I being few in number, they shall gather themselves together against me, and slay me; and I shall be destroyed, I and my house. ³¹And they said, Should he deal with our sister as with an harlot?

 **A**nd it came to pass when Joseph was come unto his brethren, that they stripped Joseph out of his coat, his coat of many colors that was on him; ²⁴And they took him, and cast him into a pit: and the pit was empty, there was no water in it. ²⁵And they sat down to eat bread: and they lifted up their eyes and looked, and, behold, a company of Ishmeelites came from Gilead with their camels bearing spicery and balm and myrrh, going to carry it down to Egypt. ²⁶And Judah said unto his brethren, What profit is it if we slay our brother, and conceal his blood? ²⁷Come, and let us sell him to the Ishmeelites, and let not our hand be upon him; for he is our brother and our flesh. And his brethren were content. ²⁸Then there passed by Midianites merchantmen; and they drew and lifted up Joseph out of the pit, and sold Joseph to the Ishmeelites for twenty pieces of silver; and they brought Joseph into Egypt. ²⁹And Reuben returned unto the pit; and, behold, Joseph was not in the pit; and he rent his clothes. ³⁰And he returned unto his brethren, and said, The child is not; and I, whither shall I go? ³¹And they took Joseph's coat, and killed a kid of the goats, and dipped the coat in the blood; ³²And they sent the coat of many colors, and they brought it to their father; and said, This have we found: know now whether it be thy son's coat or no. ³³And he knew it, and said, It is my son's coat; an evil beast hath devoured him; Joseph is without doubt rent in pieces. ³⁴And Jacob rent his clothes, and put sackcloth upon his loins, and mourned for his son many days.

And in process of time the daughter of Shuah Judah's wife died; and Judah was comforted, and went up unto his sheepshearers to Timnath, he and his friend Hirah the Adullamite. ¹³And it was told Tamar, saying, Behold thy father in law goeth up to Timnath to shear his sheep. ¹⁴And she put her widow's garments off from her, and covered her with a veil, and wrapped herself, and sat in an open place, which is by the way to Timnath; for she saw that Shelah was grown, and she was not given unto him to wife. ¹⁵When Judah saw her, he thought her to be an harlot; because she had covered her face. ¹⁶And he turned unto her by the way, and said, Go to, I pray thee, let me come in unto thee; (for he knew not that she was his daugher in law.) And she said, What wilt thou give me, that thou mayest come in unto me? ¹⁷And he said, I will send thee a kid from the flock. And she said, Wilt thou give me a pledge, till thou send it? ¹⁸And he said, What pledge shall I give thee? And she said, Thy signet, and thy bracelets, and thy staff that is in thine hand. And he gave it her, and came in unto her, and she conceived by him. ¹⁹And she arose, and went away, and laid by her veil from her, and put on the garments of her widowhood.

nd it came to pass a-
bout this time, that Jo-
seph went into the
house to do his busi-
ness; and there was
none of the men of the
house there within.
[12]And she caught him by his garment, saying,
Lie with me: and he left his garment in her
hand, and fled, and got him out. [13]And it came
to pass, when she saw that he had left his garment in her hand, and was fled forth, [14]That
she called unto the men of her house, and
spake unto them, saying, See, he hath brought
in a Hebrew unto us to mock us; he came in
unto me to lie with me, and I cried with a loud
voice: [15]And it came to pass, when he heard
that I lifted up my voice and cried, that he
left his garment with me, and fled, and got
him out. [16]And she laid up his garment by her,
until his lord came home. [17]And she spake
unto him, according to these words, saying,
The Hebrew servant, which thou hast brought
unto us, came in unto me to mock me: [18]And it
came to pass, as I lifted up my voice and cried,
that he left his garment with me, and fled out.
[19]And it came to pass, when his master heard
the words of his wife, which she spake unto
him, saying, After this manner did thy servant
to me; that his wrath was kindled. [20]And Joseph's master took him, and put him into the
prison, a place where the king's prisoners were
bound: and he was there in the prison. [21]But
the LORD was with Joseph, and shewed him
mercy, and gave him favor in the sight of the
keeper of the prison. [22]And the keeper of the
prison committed to Joseph's hand all the
prisoners that were in the prison; and whatsoever they did there, he was the doer of it.
[23]The keeper of the prison looked not to any
thing that was under his hand; because the
LORD was with him, and that which he did, the
LORD made it to prosper.

hen Pharaoh sent and called Joseph, and they brought him hastily out of the dungeon: and he shaved himself, and changed his raiment, and came in unto Pharaoh. [15]And Pharaoh said unto Joseph, I have dreamed a dream, and there is none that can interpret it: and I have heard say of thee, that thou canst understand a dream to interpret it. [16]And Joseph answered Pharaoh, saying, It is not in me: God shall give Pharaoh an answer of peace.

ow when Jacob saw that there was corn in Egypt, Jacob said unto his sons, Why do ye look one upon another? [2]And he said, Behold, I have heard that there is corn in Egypt: get you down thither, and buy for us from thence; that we may live, and not die. [3]And Joseph's ten brethren went down to buy corn in Egypt. [4]But Benjamin, Joseph's brother, Jacob sent not with his brethren; for he said, Lest peradventure mischief befall him. [5]And the sons of Israel came to buy corn among those that came: for the famine was in the land of Canaan.

nd Joseph was the governor over the land, and he it was that sold to all the people of the land: and Joseph's brethren came, and bowed down themselves before him with their faces to the earth. [7]And Joseph saw his brethren, and he knew them, but made himself strange unto them, and spake roughly unto them; and he said unto them, Whence come ye? And they said, From the land of Canaan to buy food. [8]And Joseph knew his brethren, but they knew not him. [9]And Joseph remembered the dreams which he dreamed of them, and said unto them, Ye are spies; to see the nakedness of the land ye are come. [10]And they said unto him, Nay, my lord, but to buy food are thy servants come. [11]We are all one man's sons; we are true men, thy servants are no spies. [12]And he said unto them, Nay, but to see the nakedness of the land ye are come. [13]And they said, Thy servants are twelve brethren, the sons of one man in the land of Canaan; and, behold, the youngest is this day with our father, and one is not. [14]And Joseph said unto them, That is it that I spake unto you, saying, Ye are spies: [15]Hereby ye shall be proved: By the life of Pharaoh ye shall not go forth hence; except your youngest brother come hither. [16]Send one of you, and let him fetch your brother, and ye shall be kept in prison, that your words may be proved, whether there be any truth in you: or else by the life of Pharaoh surely ye are spies. [17]And he put them all together into ward three days.

And they made ready the present against Joseph came at noon: for they heard that they should eat bread there. [26]And when Joseph came home, they brought him the present which was in their hand into the house, and bowed themselves to him to the earth. [27]And he asked them of their welfare, and said, Is your father well, the old man of whom ye spake? Is he yet alive? [28]And they answered, Thy servant our father is in good health, he is yet alive. And they bowed down their heads, and made obeisance. [29]And he lifted up his eyes, and saw his brother Benjamin, his mother's son, and said, Is this your younger brother, of whom ye spake unto me? And he said, God be gracious unto thee, my son. [30]And Joseph made haste; for his bowels did yearn upon his brother: and he sought where to weep; and he entered into his chamber, and wept there. [31]And he washed his face, and went out, and refrained himself, and said, Set on bread. [32]And they set on for him by himself, and for them by themselves, and for the Egyptians, which did eat with him, by themselves: because the Egyptians might not eat bread with the Hebrews; for that is an abomination unto the Egyptians. [33]And they sat before him, the firstborn according to his birthright, and the youngest according to his youth: and the men marvelled one at another. [34]And he took and sent messes unto them from before him: but Benjamin's mess was five times so much as any of theirs. And they drank, and were merry with him.

nd the king of Egypt spake to the Hebrew midwives, of which the name of the one was Shiphrah, and the name of the other Puah: ¹⁶And he said, When ye do the office of a midwife to the Hebrew women, and see them upon the stools; if it be a son, then ye shall kill him: but if it be a daughter, then she shall live. ¹⁷But the midwives feared God, and did not as the king of Egypt commanded them, but saved the men children alive. ¹⁸And the king of Egypt called for the midwives, and said unto them, Why have ye done this thing, and have saved the men children alive? ¹⁹And the midwives said unto Pharaoh, Because the Hebrew women are not as the Egyptian women; for they are lively, and are delivered ere the midwives come in unto them. ²⁰Therefore God dealt well with the midwives: and the people multiplied, and waxed very mighty. ²¹And it came to pass, because the midwives feared God, that he made them houses. ²²And Pharaoh charged all his people, saying, Every son that is born ye shall cast into the river, and every daughter ye shall save alive.

nd there went a man of the house of Levi, and took to wife a daughter of Levi. [2]And the woman conceived, and bare a son: and when she saw him that he was a goodly child, she hid him three months. [3]And when she could not longer hide him, she took for him an ark of bulrushes, and daubed it with slime and with pitch, and put the child therein; and she laid it in the flags by the river's brink. [4]And his sister stood afar off, to wit what would be done to him. [5]And the daughter of Pharaoh came down to wash herself at the river; and her maidens walked along by the river's side; and when she saw the ark among the flags, she sent her maid to fetch it. [6]And when she had opened it, she saw the child: and, behold, the babe wept. And she had compassion on him, and said, This is one of the Hebrew's children. [7]Then said his sister to Pharaoh's daughter, Shall I go and call to thee a nurse of the Hebrew women, that she may nurse the child for thee? [8]And Pharaoh's daughter said to her, Go. And the maid went and called the child's mother. [9]And Pharaoh's daughter said unto her, Take this child away, and nurse it for me, and I will give thee thy wages. And the woman took the child, and nursed it. [10]And the child grew, and she brought him unto Phar-aoh's daughter, and he became her son. And she called his name Moses: and she said, Because I drew him out of the water.

ow Moses kept the flock of Jethro his father in law, the priest of Midian: and he led the flock to the backside of the desert, and came to the mountain of God, even to Horeb. ²And the angel of the LORD appeared unto him in a flame of fire out of the midst of a bush: and he looked with fire, and the bush was not consumed. ³And Moses said, I will now turn aside, and see this great sight, why the bush is not burnt. ⁴And when the LORD saw that he turned aside to see, God called unto him out of the midst of the bush, and said, Moses, Moses. And he said, Here am I. ⁵And he said, Draw not nigh hither: put off thy shoes from off thy feet, for the place whereon thou standest is holy ground. ⁶Moreover he said, I am the God of thy father, the god of Abraham, the God of Isaac, and the God of Jacob. And Moses hid his face; for he was afraid to look upon God. ⁷And the LORD said, I have surely seen the affliction of my people which are in Egypt, and have heard their cry by reason of their taskmasters; for I know their sorrows; ⁸And I am come down to deliver them out of the hand of the Egyptians, and to bring them up out of that land unto a good land and a large, unto a land flowing with milk and honey; unto the place of the Canaanites, and the Hittites, and the Amorites, and the Perizzites, and the Hivites, and the Jeb-u-sites. ⁹Now therefore, behold, the cry of the children of Israel is come unto me: and I have also seen the oppression wherewith the Egyptians oppress them. ¹⁰Come now therefore, and I will send thee unto Pharaoh, that thou mayest bring forth my people the children of Israel out of Egypt.

nd the LORD spake unto Moses and unto Aaron, saying, [9]When Pharaoh shall speak unto you, saying, Shew a miracle for you: then thou shalt say unto Aaron, Take thy rod, and cast it before Pharaoh, and it shall become a serpent. [10]And Moses and Aaron went in unto Pharaoh, and they did so as the LORD had commanded: and Aaron cast down his rod before Pharaoh, and before his servants, and became a serpent. [11]Then Pharaoh also called the wise men and the sorcerers: now the magicians of Egypt, they also did in like manner with their enchantments. [12]For they cast down every man his rod, and they became serpents: but Aaron's rod swallowed up their rods. [13]And he hardened Pharaoh's heart, that he hearkened not unto them; as the LORD had said.

nd the LORD spake unto Moses, Go unto Pharaoh, and say unto him, Thus saith the LORD, Let my people go, that they may serve me. ²And if thou refuse to let them go, behold, I will smite all thy borders with frogs: ³And the river shall bring forth frogs abundantly, which shall go up and come into thine house, and into thy bedchamber, and upon thy bed, and into the house of thy servants, and upon thy people, and into thine ovens, and into thy kneadingtroughs: ⁴And the frogs shall come up both on thee, and upon thy people, and upon all thy servants. ⁵And the LORD spake unto Moses, Say unto Aaron, Stretch forth thine hand with thy rod over the streams, over the rivers, and over the ponds, and cause frogs to come up upon the land of Egypt. ⁶And Aaron stretched out his hand over the waters of Egypt; and the frogs came up, and covered the land of Egypt. ⁷And the magicians did so with their enchantments, and brought up frogs upon the land of Egypt. ⁸Then Pharaoh called for Moses and Aaron, and said, Entreat the LORD, that he may take away the frogs from me, and from my people; and I will let the people go, that they may do sacrifice unto the LORD. ⁹And Moses said unto Pharaoh, Glory over me: when shall I entreat for thee, and for thy servants, and for thy people, to destroy the frogs from thee and thy houses, that they may remain in the river only? ¹⁰And he said, Tomorrow. And he said, Be it according to thy word: that thou mayest know that there is none like unto the LORD our God. ¹¹And the frogs shall depart from thee, and from thy houses, and from thy servants, and from thy people; they shall remain in the river only.

nd the Lord spake unto Moses and Aaron in the land of Egypt, saying, [2]This month shall be unto you the beginning of months: it shall be the first month of the year to you. [3]Speak ye unto all the congregation of Israel, saying, In the tenth day of this month they shall take to them every man a lamb, according to the house of their fathers, a lamb for an house: [4]And if the household be too little for the lamb, let him and his neighbor next unto his house take it according to the number of the souls; every man according to his eating shall make your count for the lamb. [5]Your lamb shall be without blemish, a male of the first year: ye shall take it out from the sheep, or from the goats: [6]And ye shall keep it up until the fourteenth day of the same month: and the whole assembly of the congregation of Israel shall kill it in the evening. [7]And they shall take of the blood, and strike it on the two side posts and on the upper door post of the houses, wherein they shall eat it. [8]And they shall eat the flesh in that night, roast with fire, and unleavened bread; and with bitter herbs they shall eat it. [9]Eat not of it raw, nor sodden at all with water, but roast with fire; his head with his legs, and with the purtenance thereof. [10]And ye shall let nothing of it remain until the morning; and that which remaineth of it until the morning ye shall burn with fire. [11]And thus shall ye eat it; with your loins girded, your shoes on your feet, and your staff in your hand; and ye shall eat it in haste: it is the Lord's passover.

And Moses stretched out his hand over the sea; and the LORD caused the sea to go back by a strong east wind all that night, and made the sea dry land, and the waters were divided. ²²And the children of Israel went into the midst of the sea upon the dry ground: and the waters were a wall unto them on their right hand, and on their left. ²³And the Egyptians pursued, and went in after them to the midst of the sea, even all Pharaoh's horses, his chariots, and his horsemen. ²⁴And it came to pass, that in the morning watch the LORD looked unto the host of the Egyptians through the pillar of fire and of the cloud, and troubled the host of the Egyptians, ²⁵And took off their chariot wheels, that they drave them heavily: so that the Egyptians said, Let us flee from the face of Israel; for the LORD fighteth for them against the Egyptians. ²⁶And the LORD said unto Moses, Stretch out thine hand over the sea, that the waters may come again upon the Egyptians, upon their chariots, and upon their horsemen. ²⁷And Moses stretched forth his hand over the sea, and the sea returned to his strength when the morning appeared; and the Egyptians fled against it; and the LORD overthrew the Egyptians in the midst of the sea. ²⁸And the waters returned, and covered the chariots, and the horsemen, and all the host of Pharaoh that came into the sea after them; there remained not so much as one of them. ²⁹But the children of Israel walked upon dry land in the midst of the sea; and the waters were a wall unto them on their right hand, and on their left. ³⁰Thus the LORD saved Israel that day out of the hand of the Egyptians; and Israel saw the Egyptians dead upon the sea shore. ³¹And Israel saw that great work which the LORD did upon the Egyptians: and the people feared the LORD, and his servant Moses.

hen came Amalek, and fought with Israel in Rephidim. [9]And Moses said unto Joshua, Choose us out men, and go out, fight with Amalek: tomorrow I will stand on the top of the hill with the rod of God in mine hand. [10]So Joshua did as Moses had said to him, and fought with Amalek: and Moses, Aaron, and Hur went up to the top of the hill. [11]And it came to pass, when Moses held up his hand, that Israel prevailed: and when he let down his had, Amalek prevailed. [12]But Moses's hands were heavy; and they took a stone, and put it under him, and he sat thereon; and Aaron and Hur stayed up his hands, the one on the one side, and the other on the other side; and his hands were steady until the going down of the sun. [13]And Joshua discomfited Amalek and his people with the edge of the sword. [14]And the LORD said unto Moses, Write this for a memorial in a book, and rehearse it in the ears of Joshua: for I will utterly put out the remembrance of Amalek from under heaven. [15]And Moses built an altar, and called the name of it Jehovahnissi: [16]For he said, Because the LORD hath sworn that the LORD will have war with Amalek from generation to generation.

nd it came to pass on the third day in the morning, that there were thunders and lightnings, and a thick cloud upon the mount, and the voice of the trumpet exceeding loud: so that all the people that was in the camp trembled. [17]And Moses brought forth the people out of the camp to meet with God; and they stood at the nether part of the mount. [18]And mount Sinai was altogether on a smoke thereof ascended as the smoke of a furnace, and the whole mount quaked greatly. [19]And when the voice of the trumpet sounded long, and waxed louder and louder, Moses spake, and God answered him by a voice. [20]And the LORD came down upon mount Sinai, on the top of the mount: and the LORD called Moses up to the top of the mount; and Moses went up. [21]And the LORD said unto Moses, Go down, charge the people, lest they break through unto the LORD to gaze, and many of them perish. [22]And let the priests also, which come near to the LORD, sanctify themselves, lest the LORD break forth upon them. [23]And Moses said unto the LORD, The people cannot come up to mount Sinai: for thou chargedst us, saying, Set bounds about the mount, and sanctify it. [24]And the LORD said unto him, Away, get thee down, and thou shalt come up, thou, and Aaron with thee: but let not the priests and the people break through to come up unto the LORD, lest he break forth upon them. [25]So Moses went down unto the people, and spake unto them.

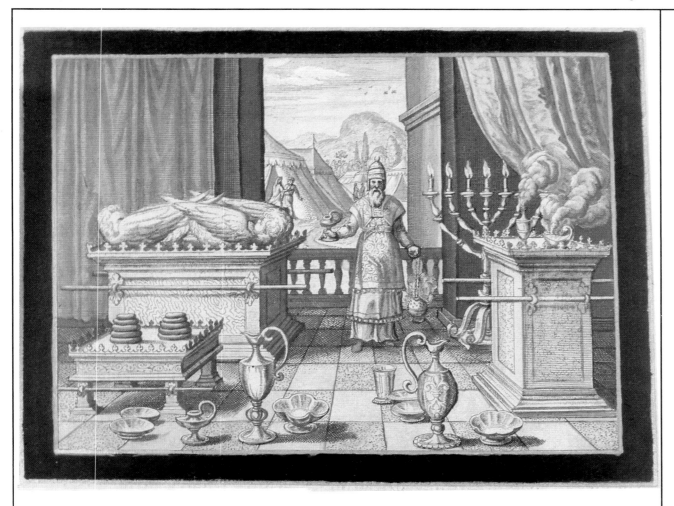

nd thou shalt make a plate of pure gold, and grave upon it, like the engravings of a signet, HOLINESS TO THE LORD. [37]And thou shalt put it on a blue lace, that it may be upon the mitre; upon the forefront of the mitre it shall be. [38]And it shall be upon Aaron's forehead, that Aaron may bear the iniquity of the holy things, which the children of Israel shall hallow in all their holy gifts; and it shall be always upon his forehead, that they may be accepted before the LORD. [39]And thou shalt embroider the coat of fine linen, and thou shalt make the mitre of fine linen, and thou shalt make the girdle of needlework. [40]And for Aaron's sons thou shalt make coats, and thou shalt make for them girdles, and bonets shalt thou make for them, for glory and for beauty. [41]And thou shalt put them upon Aaron thy brother, and his sons with him; and shalt anoint them, and con-secrate them, and sanctify them, that they may minister unto me in the priest's office. [42]And thou shalt make them linen breeches to cover their nakedness; from the loins even unto the thighs they shall reach: [43]And they shall be upon Aaron, and upon his sons, when they come in unto the tabernacle of the congregation, or when they come near unto the altar to minister in the holy place; that they bear not iniquity, and die: it shall be a statute for ever unto him and his seed after him.

nd Moses turned, and went down from the mount, and the two tables of the testimony were in his hand: the tables were written on both their sides; on the one side and on the other were they written. ¹⁶And the tables were the work of God, and the writing was the writing of God, graven upon the tables. ¹⁷And when Joshua heard the noise of the people as they shouted, he said unto Moses, There is a noise of war in the camp. ¹⁸And he said, It is not the voice or them that shout for mastery, neither is it the voice of them that cry for being overcome: but the noise of them that sing do I hear. ¹⁹And it came to pass, as soon as he came nigh unto the camp, that he saw the calf, and the dancing: and Moses' anger waxed hot, and he cast the tables out of his hands, and brake them beneath the mount. ²⁰And he took the calf which they had made, and burnt it in the fire, and ground it to powder, and strawed it upon the water, and made the children of Israel drink of it. ²¹And Moses said unto Aaron, What did this people unto thee, that thou hast brought so great a sin upon them? ²²And Aaron said, Let not the anger of my lord wax hot: thou knowest the people, that they are set on mischief. ²³For they said unto me, Make us gods, which shall go before us: for as for this Moses, the man that brought us up out of the land of Egypt, we wot not what is become of him. ²⁴And I said unto the, Whosoever hath any gold, let them break it off. So they gave it me: then I cast it into the fire, and there came out this calf.

And Nadab and Abihu, the sons of Aaron, took either of them his censer, and put fire therin, and put incense theron, and offered strange fire before the LORD, which he commanded them not. ²And there went out fire from the LORD, and devoured them, and they died before the LORD. ³Then Moses said unto Aaron, This is it that be LORD spake, saying, I will be sanctified in them that come nigh me, and before all the people I will be glorified. And Aaron held his peace. ⁴And Moses called Mishel and Elzaphan, the sons of Uzziel the uncle of Aaron, and said unto them, Come near, carry your brethren from before the sanctuary out of the camp. ⁵So they went near, and carried them in their coats out of the camp; as Moses had said. ⁶And Moses said unto Aaron, and unto Eleazar and unto Ithamar, his sons, Uncover not your heads, neither rend your clothes; lest ye die, and lest wrath come upon all the people: but let your brethren, the whole ouse of Israel, bewail the burning which the LORD hath kindled. ⁷And ye shall not go out from the door of the tabernacle of the congregation, lest ye die: for the anointing oil of the LORD is upon you. And they did according to the word of Moses.

nd they returned from searching of the land after forty days. ²⁶And they went and came to Moses, and to Aaron, and to all the congregation of the children of Israel, unto the wilderness of Paran, to Kadesh; and brought back word unto them, and unto all the congregation, and shewed them the fruit of the land. ²⁷And they told him, and said, We came unto the land whither thou sentest us, and surely it floweth with milk and honey; and this is the fruit of it. ²⁸Nevertheless the people be strong that dwell in the land, and the cities are walled, and very great; and moreover we saw the children of Anak there. ²⁹The Amalekites dwell in the land of the south: and the Hittites, and the Jebusites, and the Amorites, dwell in the mountains: and the Canaanites dwell by the sea, and by the coast of Jordan. ³⁰And Caleb stilled the people before Moses, and said, Let us go up at once, and possess it; for we are well able to overcome it. ³¹But the men that went up with him said, We be not able to go up against the people; for they are stronger than we. ³²And they brought up an evil report of the land which they had searched unto the children of Israel, saying, The land, through which we have gone to search it, is a land that eateth up the inhabitants thereof; and all the people that we saw in it are men of a great stature. ³³And there we saw the giants, the sons of Anak, which come of the giants: and we were in our own sight as grasshoppers, and so we were in their sight.

hen came the children of Israel, even the whole congregation, into the desert of Zin in the first month: and the people abode in Kadesh; and Miriam died there, and was buried there. ²And there was no water for the congregation: and they gathered themselves together against Moses and against Aaron. ³And the people chode with Moses, and spake, saying, Would God that we had died when our brethren died before the LORD ⁴And why have ye brought up the congregation of the LORD into this wilderness, that we and our cattle should die there? ⁵And wherefore have ye made us to come up out of Egypt, to bring us in unto this evil place? it is no place of seed, or of figs, or of vines, or of pomegranates; neither is there any water to drink. ⁶And Moses and Aaron went from the presence of the assembly unto the door of the tabernacle of the congragation, and they fell upon their faces: and the glory of the LORD appeared unto them. ⁷And the LORD spake unto Moses, saying, ⁸Take the rod, and gather thou the assembly together, thou, and Aaron thy brother, and speak ye unto the rock before their eyes; and it shall give forth to them water out of the rock: so thou shalt give the congregation and their beasts drink. ⁹And Moses took the rod from before the LORD, as he commanded him. ¹⁰And Moses and Aaron gathered the congregation together before the rock, and he said unto them, Hear now, ye rebels; must we fetch you water our of this rock? ¹¹And Moses lifted up his hand, and with his rod he smote the rock twice: and the water came out abundantly, and the congregation drank, and their beasts also.

And when king Arad the Canaanite, which dwelt in the south, heard tell that Israel came by the way of the spies; then he fought against Israel, and took some of them prisoners. [2]And Israel vowed a vow unto the LORD, and said, If thou wilt indeed deliver this people into my hand, then I will utterly destroy their cities. [3]And the LORD hearkened to the voice of Israel, and delivered up the Canaanites; and they utterly destroyed them and their cities: and he called the name of the place Hormah. [4]And they journeyed from mount Hor by the way of the Red Sea, to compass the land of Edom and the soul of the people was much discouraged because of the way. [5]And the people spake against God, and against Moses, Wherefore have ye brought us up out of Egypt to die in the wilderness? for there is no bread, neither is there any water; and our soul loatheth this light bread.

[6]And the LORD sent fiery serpents among the people, and they bit the people; and much people of Israel died. [7]Therefore the people came to Moses, and said, We have sinned, for we have spoken against the LORD, that he take away the serpents from us. And Moses prayed for the people. [8]And the LORD said unto Moses, Make thee a fiery serpent, and set it upon a pole: and it shall come to pass, that every one that is bitten, when he looketh upon it, shall live. [9]And Moses made a serpent of brass, and put it upon a pole, and it came to pass, that if a serpent had bitten any man, when he beheld the serpent of brass, he lived.

nd Balaam rose up in the morning, and saddled his ass, and went with the princes of Moab. [22]And God's anger was kindled because he went: and the angel of the Lord stood in the way for an adversary against him. Now he was riding upon his ass, and his two servants were with him. [23]And the ass saw the angel of the Lord standing in the way, and his sword drawn in his hand: and the ass turned aside out of the way, and went into the field: and Balaam smote the ass, to turn her into the way. [24]But the angel of the Lord stood in a path of the vineyards, a wall being on this side, and a wall on that side. [25]And when the ass saw the angel of the Lord, she thrust herself unto the wall, and crushed Balaam's foot against the wall: and he smote her again. [26]And the angel of the Lord went further, and stood in a narrow place, where was no way to turn either to the right hand or to the left. [27]And when the ass saw the angel of the Lord, she fell down under Balaam: and Balaam's anger was kindled, and he smote the ass with a staff. [28]And the Lord opened the mouth of the ass, and she said unto Balaam, What have I done unto thee, thou hast smitten me these three times? [29]And Balaam said unto the ass, Because thou hast mocked me: I would there were a sword in mine hand, for now would I kill thee. [30]And the ass said unto Balaam, Am not I thine ass, upon which thou hast ridden·ever since I was thine unto this day? Was I ever wont to do so unto thee? And he said, nay. [31]Then the Lord opened the eyes of Balaam, and he saw the angel of the Lord standing in the way, and his sword drawn in his hand: and he bowed down his head, and fell flat on his face.

nd Moses went up from the plains of Moab unto the mountain of Nebo, to the top of Pisgah, that is over against Jericho. And the Lord shewed him all the land of Gilead, unto Dan, [2]And all Naphtali, and the land of Ephraim, an Manasseh, and all the land of Judah, unto the utmost sea, [3]And the south, and the plain of the valley of Jericho, the city of palm trees, unto Zoar. [4]And the Lord said unto him, This is the land which I sware unto Abraham, unto Isaac, and unto Jacob, saying, I will give it unto thy seed: I have caused thee to see it with thine eyes, but thou shalt not go over thither. [5]So Moses the servant of the Lord died there in the land of Moab, according to the word of the Lord. [6]And he buried him in a valley in the land of Moab, over against Bethpeor: but no man knoweth of his sepulchre unto this day.

nd Joshua said unto the children of Israel, Come hither, and hear the words of the LORD your God. [10]And Joshua said, Hereby ye shall know that the living God is among you, and that he will without fail drive out from before you the Canaanites, and the Hittites, and the Hivites, and the Perizzites, and the Girgashites, and the Amorites, and the Jebusites. [11]Behold, the ark of the covenant of the LORD of all the earth passeth over before you into Jordan. [12]Now therefore take you twelve men out of the tribes of Israel, out of every tribe a man. [13]And it shall come to pass, as soon as the soles of the feet of the priests that bear the ark of the LORD, the LORD of all the earth, shall rest in the waters of Jordan, that the waters of Jordan shall be cut off from the waters that come down from above; and they shall stand upon a heap. [14]And it came to pass, when the people removed from their tents, to pass over Jordan, and the priests bearing the ark of the covenant before the people; [15]And as they that bare the ark were come unto Jordan, and the feet of the priests that bare the ark were dipped in the brim of the water, (for Jordan overfloweth all his banks all the time of harvest,) [16]That the waters which came down from above stood and rose up upon an heap very far from the city Adam, that is beside Zaretan: and those that came down toward the sea of the plain, even the salt sea, failed, and were cut off: and the people passed over right against Jericho. [17]And the priests that bare the ark of the covenant of the LORD stood firm on dry ground in the midst of Jordan, and all the Israelites passed over on dry ground, until all the people were passed clean over Jordan.

nd it came to pass on the seventh day, that they rose early about the dawning of the day, and compassed the city after the same manner seven times: only on that day they compassed the city seven times. [16]And it came to pass at the seventh time, when the priests blew with the trumpets, Joshua said unto the people, Shout; for the LORD hath given you the city. [17]And the city shall be acursed, even it, and all that are therein, to the LORD: only Rahab the harlot shall live, she and all that are with her in the house, because she hid the messengers that we sent. [18]And ye, in any wise keep yourselves from the accursed thing, lest ye make yourselves accursed, when ye take of the accursed thing, and make the camp of Israel a curse, and trouble it. [19]But all the silver, and gold, and vessels of brass and iron, are consecrated unto the LORD: they shall come into the treasury of the LORD. [20]So the people shouted when the priests blew with the trumpets: and it came to pass, when the people heard the sound of the trumpet, and the people shouted with a great shout, that the wall fell down flat, so that the people went up into the city, every man straight before him, and they took the city. [21]And they utterly destroyed all that was in the city, both man and woman, young and old, and ox, and sheep, and ass, with the edge of the sword.

And the Lord said unto Joshua, Stretch out the spear that is in thy hand toward Ai; for I will give it into thine hand. And Joshua stretched out the spear that he had in his hand toward the city. [19]And the ambush arose quickly out of their place, and they ran as soon as he had stretched out his hand: and they entered into the city, and took it, and hasted and set the city on fire. [20]And when the men of Ai looked behind them, they saw, and, behold, the smoke of the city ascended up to heaven, and they had no power to flee this way or that way: and the people that fled to the wilderness turned back upon the pursuers. [21]And when Joshua and all Israel saw that the ambush had taken the city, and that the smoke of the city ascended, then they turned again, and slew the men of Ai. [22]And the other issued out of the city against them; so they were in the midst of Israel, some on this side, and some on that side: and they smote them, so that they let none of them remain or escape. [23]And the king of Ai they took alive, and brought him to Joshua. [24]And it came to pass, when Israel had made an end of slaying all the inhabitants of Ai in the field, in the wilderness wherein they chased them, and when they were all fallen on the edge of the sword, until they were consumed, that all the Israelites returned unto Ai, and smote it with the edge of the sword. [25]And so it was, that all that fell that day, both of men and women, were twelve thousand even all the men of Ai.

nd the men of Gibeon sent unto Joshua to the camp to Gilgal, saying, Slack not thy hand from thy servants; come up to us quickly, and save us, and help us: for all the kings of the Amorites that dwell in the mountains are gathered together against us. [7]So Joshua ascended from Gilgal, he, and all the people of war with him, and all the mighty men of valor. [8]And the LORD said unto Joshua, Fear them not: for I have delivered them into thine hand; there shall not a man of them stand before thee. [9]Joshua therefore came unto them suddenly, and went up from Gilgal all night. [10]And the LORD discomfited them before Israel, and slew them with a great slaughter at Gibeon, and chased them along the way that goeth up to Bethhoron, and smote them to Azekah, and unto Makkedah. [11]And it came to pass, as they fled from before Israel, and were in the going down to Beth-horon, that the LORD cast down great stones from heaven upon them unto Azekah, and they died: they were more which died with hailstones than they whom the children of Israel slew with the sword. [12]Then spake Joshua to the LORD in the day when the LORD delivered up the Amorites before the children of Israel, and he said in the sight of Israel, Sun, stand thou still upon Gibeon; and thou, Moon, in the valley of Ajalon. [13]And the sun stood still, and the moon stayed, until the people had avenged themselves upon their enemies. Is not this written in the book of Jasher? So the sun stood still in the midst of heaven, and hasted not to go down about a whole day. [14]And there was no day like that before it or after it, that the LORD fought for Israel. [15]And Joshua returned, and all Israel with him, unto the camp to Gilgal.

And it came to pass, when Jabin king of Hazor had heard those things, that he sent to Jobab king of Madon, and to the king of Shimron, and to the king of Achshaph, [2]And to the kings that were on the north of the mountains, and of the plains south of Chin-ne-roth, and in the valley, and in the borders of Dor on the west, [3]And to the Canaanite on the east and on the west, and to the Amorite, and the Hittite, and the Perizzite, and the Jebusite in the mountains, and to the Hivite under Hermon in the land of Mizpeh. [4]And they went out, they and all their hosts with them, much people, even as the sand that is upon the sea shore in multitude, with horses and chariots very many. [5]And when all these kings were met together, they came and pitched together at the waters of Merom, to fight against Israel. [6]And the LORD said unto Joshua, Be not afraid because of

them: for tomorrow about this time will I deliver them up all slain before Israel: thou shalt hock their horses, and burn their chariots with fire. [7]So Joshua came, and all the people of war with him, against them by the waters of Merom suddenly; and they fell upon them. [8]And the LORD delivered them into the hand of Israel, who smote them, and chased them unto great Zidon, and unto Misrephothmaim, and unto the valley of Mizpeh eastward; and they smote them, until they left them none remaining. [9]And Joshua did unto them as the LORD bade him: he hocked their horses, and burnt their chariots with fire. [10]And Joshua at that time turned back, and took Hazor, and smote the king thereof with the sword: for Hazor beforetime was the head of all those kingdoms. [11]And they smote all the souls that were therein with the edge of the sword, utterly destroying them: there was not any left to breathe: and he burnt Hazor with fire.

ow after the death of Joshua it came to pass, that the children of Israel asked the Lord, saying, Who shall go up for us against the Canaanites first, to fight against them? ²And the Lord said, Judah shall go up: behold, I have delivered the land into his hand. ³And Judah said unto Simeon his brother, Come up with me into my lot, that we may fight against the Canaanites; and I likewise will go with thee into thy lot. So Simeon went with him. ⁴And Judah went up; and the Lord delivered the Canaanites and the Perizzites into their hand: and they slew of them in Bezek ten thousand men. ⁵And they found Adonibezek in Bezek: and they fought against him, and they slew the Canaanites and the Perizzites. ⁶But Adonibezek fled; and they pursued after him, and caught him, and cut off his thumbs and his great toes. ⁷And Adonibezek said, Threescore and ten kings, having their thumbs and their great toes cut off, gathered their meat under my table: as I have done, so God hath requited me. And they brought him to Jerusalem, and there he died. ⁸Now the children of Judah had fought against Jerusalem, and had taken it, and smitten it with the edge of the sword, and set the city on fire. ⁹And afterward the children of Judah went down to fight against the Canaanites, that dwelt in the mountain, and in the south, and in the valley.

owbeit Sisera fled away on his feet to the tent of Jael the wife of Heber the Kenite: for there was peace between Jabin the king of Hazor and the house of Heber the Kenite. [18]And Jael went out to meet Sisera, and said unto him, Turn in, my lord, turn in to me; fear not. And when he had turned in unto her into the tent, she covered him with a mantle. [19]And he said unto her, Give me, I pray thee, a little water to drink; for I am thirsty. And she opened a bottle of milk, and gave him drink, and covered him. [20]Again he said unto her, Stand in the door of the tent, and it shall be, when any man doth come and inquire of thee, and say, Is there any man here? that thou shalt say, No. [21]Then Jael Heber's wife took a nail of the tent, and took an hammer in her hand, and went softly unto him, and smote the nail into his temples, and fastened it into the ground: for he was fast asleep and weary.

So he died. [22]And, behold, as Barak pursued Sisera, Jael came out to meet him, and said unto him, Come, and I will shew thee the man whom thou seekest. And when he came into her tent, behold, Sisera lay dead, and the nail was in his temples. [23]So God subdued on that day Jabin the king of Canaan before the children of Israel. [24]And the hand of the children of Israel prospered, and prevailed against Jabin the king of Canaan, until they had destroyed Jabin king of Canaan.

nd the LORD looked upon him, and said, Go in this thy might, and thou shalt save Israel from the hand of the Midianites: have not I sent thee? ¹⁵And he said unto him, Oh my LORD, wherewith shall I save Israel? behold, my family is poor in Manasseh, and I am the least in my father's house. ¹⁶And the LORD said unto him, Surely I will be with thee, and thou shalt smite the Midianites as one man. ¹⁷And he said unto him, If now I have found grace in thy sight, then shew me a sign that thou talkest with me. ¹⁸Depart not hence, I pray thee, until I come unto thee, and bring forth my present, and set it before thee. And he said, I will tarry until thou come again. ¹⁹And Gideon went in, and made ready a kid, an unleavened cakes of an Ephah of flour: the flesh he put in a basket, and he put the broth in a pot, and brought it out unto him under the oak, and presented it. ²⁰And the angel of God said unto him, Take the flesh and the unleavened cakes, and lay them upon this rock, and pour out the broth. And he did so. ²¹Then the angel of the LORD put forth the end of the staff that was in his hand, and touched the flesh and the unleavened cakes; and there rose up fire out of the rock, and consumed the flesh and the unleavened cakes. Then the angel of the LORD departed out of his sight. ²²And when Gideon perceived that he was an angel of the LORD, Gideon said, Alas, O LORD God! for because I have seen an angel of the LORD face to face. ²³And the LORD said unto him, Peace be unto thee; fear not: thou shalt not die. ²⁴Then Gideon built an altar there unto the LORD, and called it Jehovah-shalom: unto this day it is yet in Ophrah of the Abi-ezrites.

hen Jerubbaal, who is Gideon, and all the people that were with him, rose up early, and pitched beside the well of Harod: so that the host of the Midianites were on the north side of them, by the hill of Moreh, in the valley. [2]And the LORD said unto Gideon, The people that are with thee are too many for me to give the Midianites into their hands, lest Israel vaunt themselves against me, saying, Mine own hand hath saved me. [3]Now therefore go to, proclaim in the ears of the people, saying, Whosoever is fearful and afraid, let him return and depart early from mount Gilead. And there returned of the people twenty and two thousand; and there remained ten thousand. [4]And the LORD said unto Gid-eon, The people are yet too many; bring them down unto the water, and I will try them for thee there: and it shall be, that of whom I say unto thee, This shall go with thee, the same shall go with thee; and of whomsoever I say unto thee, This shall not go with thee, the same shall not go. [5]So he brought down the people unto the water: and the LORD said unto Gideon, Every one that lappeth of the water with his tongue, as a dog lappeth, him shalt thou set by himself; likewise every one that boweth down upon his knees to drink. [6]And a number of them that lapped, putting their hand to their mouth, were three hundred men: but all the rest of the people bowed down upon their knees to drink water. [7]And the LORD said unto Gideon, By the three hundred men that lapped will I save you, and deliver the Midianites into thine hand: and let all the other people go every man unto his place. [8]So the people took victuals in their hand, and their trumpets: and he sent all the rest of Israel every man unto his tent, and retained those three hundred men: and the host of Midian was beneath him in the valley.

nd he divided the three hundred men into three companies, and he put a trumpet in every man's hand, with empty pitchers, and lamps within the pitchers. [17]And he said unto them, Look on me, and do likewise: and, behold, when I come to the outside of the camp, it shall be that, as I do, so shall ye do. [18]When I blow with a trumpet, I and all that are with me, then blow ye the trumpets also on every side of all the camp, and say, The sword of the LORD, and of Gideon. [19]So Gideon, and the hundred men that were with him, came unto the outside of the camp in the beginning of the middle watch; and they had but newly set the watch: and they blew the trumpets, and brake the pitchers that were in their hands. [20]And the three companies blew the trumpets, and brake the pitchers, and held the lamps in their left hands, and the trumpets in their right hands to blow withal:

and they cried, The sword of the LORD, and of Gideon. [21]And they stood every man in his place round about the camp: and all the host ran, and cried, and fled. [22]And the three hundred blew the trumpets, and the LORD set every man's sword against his fellow, even throughout all the host: and the host fled to Bethshittah in Zererath, and to the border of Abelmeholah, unto Tabbath.

hen went Abimelech to Thebez, and encamped against Thebez, and too, it. [51]But there was a strong tower within the city, and thither fled all the men and women, and all they of the city, and shut it to them, and gat them up to the top of the tower. [52]And Abimelech came unto the tower, and fought against it, and went hard unto the door of the tower to burn it with fire. [53]And a certain woman cast a piece of a millstone upon Abimelech's head, and all to brake his skull. [54]Then he called hastily unto the young man his armor-bearer, and said unto him, Draw thy sword, and slay me, that men say not of me, A woman slew him. And his young man thrust him through, and he died. [55]And when the men of Israel saw that Abimelech was dead, they departed every man unto his place. [56]Thus God rendered the wickedness of Abimelech, which he did unto his father, in slaying his seventy brethren: [57]And all the evil of the men of Shechem did God render upon their heads: and upon them came the curse of Jotham the son of Jerubbaal.

nd Jephthah vowed a vow unto the Lord, and said, If thou shalt without fail deliver the children of Ammon into mine hands, [31]Then it shall be, that whatsoever cometh forth of the doors of my house to meet me, when I return in peace from the children of Ammon, shall surely be the Lord's, and I will offer it up for a burnt offering. [32] Jephthah passed over unto the children of Ammon to fight against them; and the Lord delivered them into his hands. [33]And he smote them from Aroer, even twenty cities, and unto the plain of the vineyards, with a very great slaughter. Thus the children of Ammon were subdued before the children of Israel. [34]And Jephthah came to Mizpeh unto his house, and, behold, his daughter came out to meet him with timbrels and with dances: and she was his only child; beside her he had neither son nor daughter. [35]And it came to pass, when he saw her, that he rent his clothes, and said, Alas, my daughter! thou hast brought me very low, and thou art one of them that trouble me: for I have opened my mouth unto the Lord, and I cannot go back. [36]And she said unto him, My father, if thou hast opened thy mouth unto the Lord, do to me according to that which hath proceeded out of thy mouth; forasmuch as the Lord hath taken vengeance for thee of thine enemies, even of the children of Ammon. [37]And she said unto her father, Let this thing be done for me: let me alone two months, that I may go up and down upon the mountains, and bewail my virginity, I and my fellows. [38]And he said, Go. And he sent her away for two months: and she went with her companions, and bewailed her virginity upon the mountains.

And Samson went down to Timnath, and saw a woman in Timnath of the daughters of the Philistines. [2]And he came up, and told his father and his mother, and said, I have seen a woman in Timnath of the daughters of the Philistines: now therefore get her for me to wife. [3]Then his father and his mother said unto him, Is there never a woman among the daughters of thy brethren, or among all my people, that thou goest to take a wife of the uncircumcised Philistines? And Samson said unto his father, Get her for me; for she pleaseth me well. [4]But his father and his mother knew not that it was of the LORD, that he sought an occasion against the Philistines: for at that time the Philistines had dominion over Israel. [5]Then went Samson down, and his father and his mother, to Timnath, and came to the vineyards of Timnath; and, behold, a young lion roared against him. [6]And the spirit of the LORD came mightily upon him, and he rent him as he would have rent a kid, and he had nothing in his hand: but he told not his father or his mother what he had done. [7]And he went down, and talked with the woman; and she pleased Samson well. [8]And after a time he returned to take her, and he turned aside to see the carcass of the lion: and, behold, there was a swarm of bees and honey in the carcass of the lion. [9]And he took thereof in his hands, and went on eating, and came to his father and mother, and he gave them, and they did eat: but he told not them that he had taken the honey out of the carcass of the lion.

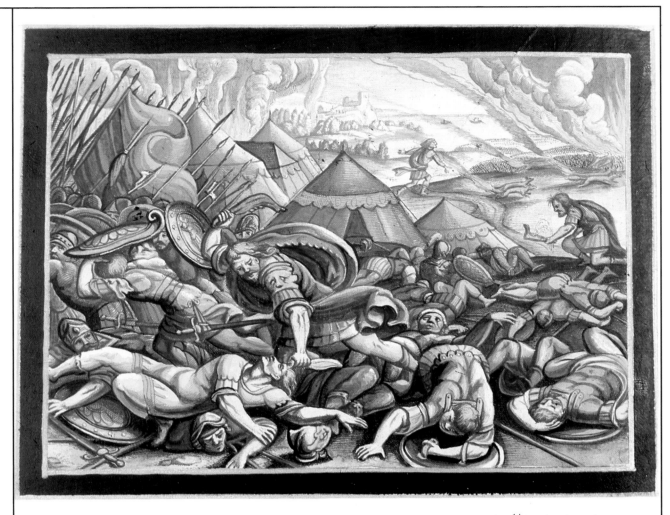

hen the Philistines went up, and pitched in Judah, and spread themselves in Lehi. ¹⁰And the men of Judah said, Why are ye come up against us? And they answered, To bind Samson are we come up, to do to him as he hath done to us. ¹¹Then three thousand men of Judah went to the top of the rock Etam, and said to Samson, Knowest thou not that the Philistines are rulers over us? What is this that thou hast done to us? And he said unto them, As they did unto me, so have I done unto them. ¹²And they said unto him, We are come down to bind thee, that we may deliver thee into the hand of the Philistines. And Samson said unto them, Swear unto me, that ye will not fall upon me yourselves. ¹³And they spake unto him, saying, No; but we will bind thee fast, and deliver thee into their hand: but surely we will not kill thee. And they bound him with two new cords, and brought him up from the rock. ¹⁴And when he came unto Lehi, the Philistines shouted against him: and the spirit of the Lᴏʀᴅ came mightily upon him, and the cords that were upon his arms became as flax that was burnt with fire, and his bands loosed from off his hands. ¹⁵And he found a new jawbone of an ass, and put forth his hand, and took it, and slew a thousand men therewith. ¹⁶And Samson said, With the jawbone of an ass, heaps upon heaps, with the jaw of an ass have I slain a thousand men.

 hen went Samson to Gaza, and saw there an harlot, and went in unto her. [2]And it was told the Gazites, saying, Samson is come hither, and they compassed him in, and laid wait for him all night in the gate of the city, and were quiet all the night, saying, In the morning, when it is day, we shall kill him. [3]And Samson lay till midnight, and arose at midnight, and took the doors of the gate of the city, and the two posts, and went away with them, bar and all, and put them upon hiss houlders, and carried them up to the top of a hill that is before Hebron.

nd when Delilah saw that he had told her all his heart, she sent and called for the lords of the Philistines, saying, Come up this once, for he hath shewed me all his heart. Then the lords of the Philistines came up unto her, and brought money in their hand. [19]And she made him sleep upon her knees; and she called for a man, and she caused him to shave off the seven locks of his head; and she began to afflict him, and his strength went from him. [20]And she said, The Philistines be upon thee, Samson. And he awoke out of his sleep, and said, I will go out as at other timesbefore, and shake myself. And he wist not that the LORD was departed from him.

[29]And Samson took hold of the two middle pillars upon which the house stook, and on which it was borne up, of the one with his right hand, and of the other with his left. [30]And Samson said, Let me die with the Philistines. And he bowed himself wit hall his might; and the house fell upon the lords, and upon all the people that were therein. So the dead which he slew at his death were more than they which he slew in his life.

nd when the men of Israel retired in the battle, Benjamin began to smite and kill of the men of Israel about thirty persons: for they said, Surely they are smitten down before us, as in the first battle. [40]But when the flame began to arise up out of the city with a pillar of smoke, the Benjamites looked behind them, and, behold, the flame of the city ascended up to heaven. [41]And when the men of Israel turned again, the men of Benjamin were amazed: for they saw that evil was come upon them. [42]Therefore they turned their backs before the men of Israel unto the way of the wilderness; but the battle overtook them; and them which came out of the cities they destroyed in the midst of them. [43]Thus they enclosed the Benjamites round about, and chased them, and trode them down with ease over against Gibeah toward the sunrising. [44]And there fell of Benjamin eighteen thousand men; all these were men of valor. [45]And they turned and fled toward the wilderness unto the rock of Rimmon: and they gleaned of them in the highways five thousand men; and pursued hard after them unto Gidom, and slew two thousand men of them. [46]So that all which fell that day of Benjamin were twenty and five thousand men that drew the sword; all these were men of valor. [47]But six hundred men turned and fled to the wilderness unto the rock Rimmon, and abode in the rock Rimmon four months. [48]And the men of Israel turned again upon the children of Benjamin, and smote them with the edge of the sword, as well the men of every city, as the beast, and all that came to hand: also they set on fire all the cities that they came to.

hen the elders of the congregation said, How shall we do for-wives for them that re-main, seeing the wo-men are destroyed out of Benjamin? [17]And they said, There must be an inheritance for them that be escaped of Benjamin, that a tribe be not destroyed out of Israel. [18]Howbeit we may not give them wives of our daughters: for the children of Israel have sworn, saying, Cur-sed be he that giveth a wife to Benjamin. [19]Then they said, Behold, there is a feast of the LORD in Shiloh yearly in a place which is on the north side of Bethel, on the east side of the highway that goeth up from Bethel to She-chem, and on the south of Lebonah. [20]There-fore they commanded the children of Benja-min, saying, Go and lie in wait in the vineyards; [21]And see, and, behold, if the daughters of Shiloh come out to dance in dances, then come you out of the vineyards, and catch you every man his wife of the daughters of Shiloh, and go to the land of Benjamin. [22]And it shall be, when their fathers ort heir brethren come unto us to complain, that we will say unto them, Be favorable unto them for our sakes: because we reserved not to each man his wife in the war: for ye did not give unto them at this time, that ye should be guilty. [23]And the children of Ben-jamin did so, and took them wives according to their number, of them that danced, whom they caught: and they went and returned unto their inheritance, and repaired the cities, and dwelt in them. [24]And the children of Israel departed thence at that time, every man to his tribe and to his family and they went out from thence every man to his inheritance. [25]In those days there was no king in Israel: every man died that which was right in his own eyes.

nd Naomi had a kinsman of her husband's, a mighty man of wealth, of the family of Elimelech; and his name was Boaz. ²And Ruth the Moabitess said unto Naomi, Let me now go to the field, and glean ears of corn after him in whose sight I shall find grace. And she said unto her, Go, my daughter. ³And she went, and came, and gleaned in the field after the reapers: and her hap was to light on a part of the field belonging unto Boaz, who was of the kindred of Elimelech. ⁴And, behold, Boaz came from Bethlehem, and said unto the reapers, The Lord be with you. And they answered him, The Lord bless thee. ⁵Then said Boaz unto his servant that was set over the reapers, Whose damsel is this? ⁶And the servant that was set over the reapers answered and said, It is the Moabitish damsel that came back with Naomi out of the country of Moab: ⁷And she said, I pray you, let me glean and gather after the reapers among the sheaves: so she came, and hath continued even from the morning until now, that she tarried a little in the house. ⁸Then said Boaz unto Ruth, Hearest thou not, my daughter? Go not to glean in another field, neither go from hence, but abide here fast by my maidens: ⁹Let thine eyes be on the field that they do reap, and go thou after them: have I not charged the young men that they shall not touch thee? and when thou art athirst, go unto the vessels, and drink of that which the young men have drawn. ¹⁰Then she fell on her face, and bowed herself to the ground, and said unto him, Why have I found grace in thine eyes, that thou shouldest take knowledge of me, seeing I am a stranger? ¹¹And Boaz answered and said unto her, It hath fully been shewed me, all that thou hast done unto thy mother in law since the death of thine husband: and how thou hast left thy father and thy mother, and the land of thy nativity, and art come unto a people which thou knewest not, heretofore.

nd there ran a man of Benjamin out of the army, and came to Shiloh the same day with his clothes rent, and with earth upon his head. [13]And when he came, lo, Eli sat upon a seat by the wayside watching: for his heart trembled for the ark of God. And when the man came into the city, and told it, all the city cried out. [14]And when Eli heard the noise of the crying, he said, What meaneth the noise of this tumult? And the man came in hastily, and told Eli. [15]Now Eli was ninety and eight years old; and his eyes were dim, that he could not see. [16]And the man said unto Eli, I am he that came out of the army, and I fled today out of the army. And he said, What is there done, my son? [17]And the messenger answered and said, Israel is fled before the Philistines, and there hath been also a great slaughter among the people, and thy two sons also, Hophni and Phinehas, are dead, and the ark of God is taken. [18]And it came to pass, when he made mention of the ark of God, that he fell from off the seat backward by the side of the gate, and his neck brake, and he died: for he was an old man, and heavy. And he had judged Israel forty years.

nd the Philistines took the ark of God, and brought it from Ebenezer unto Ashdod. ²When the Philistines took the ark of God, they brought it into the house of Dagon, and set it by Dagon. ³And when they of Ashdod arose early on the morrow, behold, Dagon was fallen upon his face to the earth before the ark of the LORD. And they took Dagon, and set him in his place again. ⁴And when they arose early on the morrow morning, behold, Dagon was fallen upon his face to the ground before the ark of the LORD; and the head of Dagon and both the psalms of his hands were cut off upon the threshold: only the stump of Dagon was left to him. ⁵Therefore neither the priests of Dagon, nor any that come into Dagons's house, tread on the threshold of Dagon in Ashdod unto this way. ⁶But the hand of the LORD was heavy upon them of Ashdold, and he destroyed them, and smote them with emerods, even Ashdod and the coasts thereof. ⁷And when the men of Ashdod saw that it was so, they said, The ark of the God of Israel shall not abide with us: for his hand is sore upon us, and upon Dagon our god. ⁸They sent therefore and gathered all the lords of the Philistines unto them, and said, What shall we do with the ark of the God of Israel be carried about unto Gath. And they carried the ark of the God of Israel about thither. ⁹And it was so, that, after they had carried it about, the hand of the LORD was against the city with a very great destruction: and he smote the men of the city, both small and great, and they had emerods in their secret parts. ¹⁰Therefore they sent the ark of God to Ekron. And it came to pass, as the ark of God came to Ekron, that the Ekronites cried out, saying, They have brought about the ark of the God of Israel to us, to slay us and our people.

And the men did so; and took two milch kine, and tied them to the cart, and shut up their calves at home: ¹¹And they laid the ark of the LORD upon the cart, and the coffer with the mice of gold and the images of their emerods. ¹²And the kine took the straight way to the way of Bethshemesh, and went along the highway, lowing as they went, and turned not aside to the right hand or to the left: and the lords of the Philistines went after them unto the border of Bethshemesh. ¹³And they of Bethshemesh were reaping their wheat harvest in the valley: and they lifted up their eyes, and saw the ark, and rejoiced to see it. ¹⁴And the cart came into the field of Joshua, a Bethshemite, and stood there, where there was a great stone: and they clave the wood of the cart, and offered the kine a burnt offering unto the LORD. ¹⁵And the Levites took down the ark of the LORD, and the coffer that was with it, wherein the jewels of gold were, and put them on the great stone: and the men of Bethshemesh offerd burnt offerings and sacrificed sacrifices the same day unto the LORD. ¹⁶And when the five lords of the Philistines had see it, they returned to Ekron the same day.

nd Samuel said, Gather all Israel to Mizpeh, and I will pray for you unto the LORD. ⁶And they gathered together to Mizpeh, and drew water, and poured it out before the LORD, and fasted on that day, and said there, We have sinned against the LORD. And Samuel judged the children of Israel in Mizpeh. ⁷And when the Philistines heard that the children of Israel were gathered together to Mizpeh, the lords of the Philistines went up against Israel. And when the children of Israel heard it, they were afraid of the Philistines. ⁸And the children of Israel said to Samuel, Cease not to cry unto the LORD our God for us, that he will save us out of the hand of the Philistines. ⁹And Samuel took a sucking lamb, and offered it for a burnt offering wholly unto the LORD: and Samuel cried unto the LORD for Israel; and the LORD heard him. ¹⁰And as Samuel was offering up the burnt offering, the Philistines drew near to battle against Israel: but the LORD thundered with a great thunder on that day upon the Philistines, and discomfited them; and they were smitten before Israel. ¹¹And the men of Israel went out of Mizpeh, and pursued the Philistines, and smote them, until they came under Bethcar. ¹²Then Samuel took a stone, and set it between Mizpeh and Shen, and called the name of it Ebenezer, saying, Hitherto hath the LORD helped us.

hen Samuel took a vial of oil, and poured it upon his head, and kissed him, and said, is it not because the LORD hath anointed thee to be captain over his inheritance? [2]When thou art departed from me to day, then thou shalt find two men by Rachel's sepulchre in the border of Benjamin at Zelzah; and they will say unto thee, The asses which thou wentest to seek are found: and, lo, thy father hath left the care of the asses, and sorroweth for you, saying, What shall I do for my son? [3]Then shalt thou go on forward from thence, and thou shalt come to the plain of Tabor, and there shall meet thee three men going up to God to Bethel, one carrying three kids, and another carrying three loaves of bread, and another carrying a bottle of wine: [4]And they will salute thee, and give thee two loaves of bread; which thou shalt receive of their hands. [5]After that thou shalt come to the hill of God, where is the garrison of the Philistines: and it shall come to pass, when thou art come thither to the city, that thou shalt meet a company of prophets coming down from the high place with a psaltery, and a tabret, and a pipe, and a harp, before them, and they shall prophesy: [6]And the spirit of the LORD will come upon thee, and thou shalt prophesy with them, and shalt be turned into another man.

nd the watchmen of Saul in Gibeah of Benjamin looked; and, behold, the multitude melted away, and they went on beating down one another. [17]Then said Saul unto the people that were with him, Number now, and see who is gone from us. And when they had numbered behold, Jonathan and his armour-bearer were not there. [18]And Saul said unto Ahiah, Bring hither the ark of God. For the ark of God was at that time with the children of Israel. [19]And it came to pass, while Saul talked unto the priest, that the noise that was in the host of the Philistines went on and increased: and Saul said unto the priest, Withdraw thine hand. [20]And Saul and all the people that were with him assembled themselves, and they came to the battle: and, behold, every man's sword was against his fellow, and there was a very great discomfiture. [21]Moreover the Hebrews that were with the Philistines before that time, which went up with them into the camp from the country round about, even they also turned to be with the Israelites that were with Saul and Jonathan. [22]Likewise all the men of Israel which-hand hid themselves in mount Ephraim, when they heard that the Philistines fled, even they also followed hard after them in the battle. [23]So the LORD saved Israel that day: and the bettle passed over unto Beth-aven.

hen said Samuel, Bring ye hither to me Agag the king of the Amalekites. And Agag came unto him delicately. And Agag said, Surely the bitterness of death is past. [33]And Samuel said, As they sword hath made women childless, so shall thy mother be childless among women. And Samuel hewed Agag in pieces before the LORD in Gilgal. [34]Then Samuel went to Ramath; and Saul went up to his house to Gibeah of Saul. [35]And Samuel came no more to see Saul until the day of his death: nevertheless Samuel mourned for Saul: and the LORD repented that he had made Saul king over Israel.

nd it came to pass, when the Philistine arose, and came and drew nigh to meet David, that David hasted, and ran toward the army to meet the Philistine. [49]And David put his hand in his bag, and took thence a stone, and slang it, and smote the Philistine in his forehead, that the stone sunk into his forehead; and he fell upon his face to the earth. [50]So David prevailed over the Philistine with a sling and with a stone, and smote the Philistine, and slew him; but there was no sword in the hand of David. [51]Therefore David ran, and stood upon the Philistine, and took his sword, and rew it out of the sheath thereof, and slew him, and cut off his head therwith. And when the Philistines saw their champion was dead, they fled.

And the men of Israel and of Judah arose, and shouted, and pursued the Philistines, until thou come to the valley, and to the gates of Ekron. And the wounded of the Philistines fell down by the way to Shaaraim, even unto Gath, and unto Ekron. [53]And the children of Israel returned from chasing after the Philistine, and they spoiled their tents. [54]And David took the head of the Philistine, and brought it to Jerusalem; but he put his armour in his tent.

nd there was war again: and David went out, and fought with the Philistines, and slew them with a great slaughter; and they fled from him. [9]And the evil spirit from the LORD was upon Saul, as he sat in his house with his javelin in his hand: and David played with his hand. [10]And Saul sought to smite David even to the wall with the javelin; but he slipped away out of Saul's presence, and he smote the javelin into the wall: and David fled, and escaped that night. [11]Saul also sent messengers unto David's house, to watch him, and to slay him in the morning: and Michal David's wife told him, saying, If thou save not thy life tonight, tomorrow thou shalt be slain. [12]So Michal let David down through a window: and he went, and fled, and escaped. [13]And Michal took an image, and laid it in the bed, and put a pillow of goats'hair for his bolster, and covered it with a cloth. [14]And when Saul sent messengers to take David, she said, He is sick. [15]And Saul sent the messengers again to see David, saying, Bring him up to me in the bed, that I may slay him. [16]And when the messengers were come in, behold, there was an image in the bed, with a pillow of goats'hair for his bolster. [17]And Saul said unto Michal, Why hast thou deceived me so, and sent away mine enemy, that he is escaped? And Michal answered Saul, He said unto me, Let me go; why should I kill thee? [18]So David fled, and escaped, and came to Samuel to Ramah, and told him all that Saul had done to him. And he and Samuel went and dwelt in Naioth.

nd it came to pass in the morning, that Jonathan went out into the field at the time appointed with David, and a little lad with him. ³⁶And he said unto his lad, Run, find out now the arrows which I shoot. And as the lad ran, he shot an arrow beyond him. ³⁷And when the lad was come to the place of the arrow which Jonathan had shot, Jonathan cried after the lad, and said, is not the arrow beyond thee? ³⁸And Jonathan cried after the lad, Make speed, haste, stay not. And Jonathan's lad gathered up the arrows, and came to his master. ³⁹But the lad knew not any thing: only Jonathan and David knew the matter. ⁴⁰And Jonathan gave his artillery unto his lad, and said unto him, Go, carry them to the city. ⁴¹And as soon as the lad was gone, David arose out of a place toward the south, and fell on his face to the ground, and bowed himself three times: and they kissed one another, and wept one with another, until David exceeded. ⁴²And Jonathan said to David, Go in peace, forasmuch as we have sworn both of us in the name of the LORD, saying, The LORD be between me and thee, and between my seed and thy seed for ever. And he arose and departed: and Jonathan went into the city.

nd when Abigail saw David, she hasted, and lighted off the ass, and fell before David on her face, and bowed herself to the ground. ²⁴And fell at his feet, and said, Upon me, my lord, upon me let this iniquity be: and let thine handmaid, I pray thee, speak in thine audience, and hear the words of thine handmaid. ²⁵Let not my LORD, I pray thee, regard this man of Belial, even Nabal: for as his name is, so is he; Nabal is his name, and folly is with him: but I thine handmaid saw not the young men of my lord, whom thou didst send. ²⁶Now therefore, my lord, as the LORD hath withholden thee form coming to shed blood, and from avenging thyself with thine own hand, now let thine enemies, and they that seek evil to my lord, be as Nabal. ²⁷And now this blessing which thine handmaid hath brought unto my lord, let it even be given unto the young men that follow my lord. ²⁸I pray thee, forgive the trespass of thine handmaid: for the LORD will certainly make my lord a sure house; because my lord fighteth the battles of the LORD, and evil hath not been found in thee all thy days. ²⁹Yet a man is risen to pursue thee, and to seek thy soul: but the soul of my lord shall be bound in the boundle of life with the LORD thy God; and the souls of thine enemies, them shall he sling out, as out of the middle of a sling. ³⁰And it shall come to pass, when the LORD shall have done to my lord according to all the good that he hath spoken concerning thee, and shall have appointed thee ruler over Israel; ³¹That this shall be no grief unto thee, nor offence of heart unto my lord, either that thou hast shed blood causeless, or that my lord hath avenged himself: but when the LORD shall have dealt well with my lord, then remember thine handmaid.

nd David arose, and came to the place where Saul had pitched: and David beheld the place where Saul lay, and Abner the son of Ner, the captain of his host: and Saul lay in the trench, and the people pitched round about him. ⁶Then answered David and said to Ahimelech the Hittite, and to Abishai the son of Zeruiah, brother to Joab, saying, Who will go down with me to Saul to the camp? And Abishai said, I will go down with thee. ⁷So David and Abishai came to the people by night: and, behold, Saul lay sleeping within the trench, and his spear stuck in the ground at his bolster: but Abner and the people lay round about him. ⁸Then said Abishai to David, God hath delivered thine enemy into thine hand this day: now therefore let me smite him, I pray thee, with the spear even to the earth at once, and I will not smite him the second time. ⁹And

David said to Abishai, Destroy him not: for who can stretch forth his hand against the Lord's anointed, and be guiltless? ¹⁰David said furthermore, As the Lord liveth, the Lord shall smite him; or his day shall come to die; or he shall descend into battle, and perish. ¹¹The Lord forbid that I should stretch forth mine hand against the Lord's anointed: but, I pray thee, take thou now the spear that is at his bolster, and the cruse of water, and let us go. ¹²So David took the spear and the cruse of water from Saul's bolster; and they gat them away, and no man saw it, nor knew it, neither awaked: for they were all asleep; because a deep sleep from the Lord was fallen upon them.

nd David was greatly distressed; for the people spake of stoning him, because the soul of all the people was grieved, every man for his sons and for his daughters: but David encouraged himself in the LORD his God. ⁷And David said to Abiathär the priest, Ahimelech's son, O pray thee, bring me hither the ephod. And Abiathar brought thither the ephod to David. ⁸And David inquired at the LORD, saying, Shall I pursue after this troop? shall I overtake them? And he answered him, Pursue: for thou shalt surely overtake them, and without fail recover all. ⁹So David went, he and the six hundred men that were with him, and came to the brook Besor, where those that were left behind stayed. ¹⁰But David pursued, he and four hundred men: for two hundred abode behind, which were so faint that they could not go over the brook Besor. ¹¹And they found an Egyptian in the field, and brought him to David, and gave him bread, and he did eat; and they made him drink water; ¹²And they gave him a piece of cake of figs, and two clusters of raisins: and when he had eaten, his spirit came again to him: for he had eaten no bread, nor drunk any water, three days and three nights. ¹³And David said unto him, To whom belongest thou? and whence art thou? And he said, I am a young man of Egypt, servant to an Amalekite; and my master left me, because three days agone I fell sick. ¹⁴We made an invasion upon the south of the Cherethites, and upon the coast which belongeth to Judah, and upon the south of Caleb; and we burned Ziklag with fire.

ow the Philistines fought against Israel: and the men of Israel fled form before the Philistines, and fell down slain in mount Gilboa. [2]And the Philistines followed hard upon Saul and upon his sons; and the Philistines slew Jonathan, and Abinadab, and Melchishua, Saul's sons. [3]And the battle went sore against Saul, and the archers hit him; and he was sore wounded of the archers. [4]Then said Saul unto his armor-bearer, Draw thy sword, and thrust me through therewith; lest these uncircumcised come and thrust me through, and abuse me. But his armor-bearer would not; for he was sore afraid. Therefore Saul took a sword, and fell upon it. [5]And when his armor-bearer saw that Saul was dead, he fell likewise upon his sword, and died with him. [6]So Saul died, and his three sons, and his armor-bearer, and all his men, that same day together. [7]And when the men of Israel that were on the other side of the valley, and they that were on the other side of Jordan, saw that the men of Israel fled, and that Saul and his sons were dead, they forsook the cities, and fled; and the Philistines came and dwelt in them.

nd it came to pass on the morrow, when the Philistines came to strip the slain, that they found Saul and his three sons fallen in the mount Gilboa. [9]And they cut off his head, and stripped off his armor, and sent into the land of the Philistines round about, to publish it in the house of their idols, and among the people. [10]And they put his armor in the house of Ashtaroth: and they fastened his body to the wall of Bethshan. [11]And when the inhabitants of Jabeshgilead heard of that which the Philistines had done to Saul; [12]All went valiant men arose, and went all night, and took the body of Saul and the bodies of his sons from the wall of Bethshan, and came to Jabesh, and burnt them there. [13]And they took their bones, and buried them under a tree at Jabesh, and fasted seven days.

And it was told king David, saying, The LORD hath blessed the house of Obededom, and all that pertaineth unto him, because of the ark of God. So David went and brought up the ark of God from the house of Obededom into the city of David with gladness. ¹³And it was so, that when they that bare the ark of the LORD had gone six paces, he sacrificed oxen and fatlings. ¹⁴And David danced before the LORD with all his might; and David was girded with a linnen e-phod. ¹⁵So David and all the house of Israel brought up the ark of the LORD with shouting, and with the sound of the trumpet. ¹⁶And as the ark of the LORD came into the city of David. Michal Saul's daughter looked through a window, and saw king David leaping and dancing before the LORD; and she despised him in her heart. ¹⁷And they brought in the ark of the LORD, and set it in his place, in the midst of the tabernacle that David had pitched for it: and David offered burnt offerings and peace offerings before the LORD. ¹⁸And as soon as David had made an end of offering burnt offerings and peace offerings, he blessed the people in the name of the LORD of the host. ¹⁹And he dealt among all the people, even among the whole multitude of Israel, as well to the women as men, to every one a cake of bread, and a good piece of flesh, and a flagon of wine. So all the people departed every one to his house.

nd the children of Ammon came out, and put the battle in array at the entering in of the gate: and the Syrians of Zoba, and of Rehob, and Ishtob, and Maacah, were by themselves in the field. ⁹When Joab saw that the front of the battle was against him before and behind, he chose of all the choice men of Israel, and put them in array against the Syrians: ¹⁰And the rest of the people he delivered into the hand of Anishai his brother, that he might put them in array against children of Ammon. ¹¹And he said, If the Syrians be too strong for me, then thou shalt help me: but if the children of Ammon be too strong for thee, then I will come and help thee. ¹²Be of good courage, and let us play the men for our people, and for the cities of our God: and the Lord do that which seemeth him good. ¹³And Joab drew nigh, and the people that were with him, unto the battle against the Syrians: and they fled before him. ¹⁴And when the children of Ammon saw that the Syrians were fled, then fled they also before Abishai, and entered into the city. So Joab returned from the children of Ammon, and came to Jerusalem. ¹⁵And when the Syrians saw that they were smitten before Israel, they gathered themselves together. ¹⁶And Hadarezer sent, and brought out the Syrians that were beyond the river: and they came to Helam; and Shobach the captain of the host of Hadarezer went before them. ¹⁷And when it was told David, he gathered all Israel together, and passed over Jordan, and came to Helam. And the Syrians set themselves in array against David, and fought with him. ¹⁸And the Syrians fled before Israel; and David slew the men of seven hundred chariots of the Syrians, and forty thousand horsemen, and smote Shobach, the captain of their host, who died there.

And it came to pass in an eveningtide, that David arose from off his bed, and walked upon the roof of the king's house: and from the roof he saw a woman washing herself; and the woman was very beautiful to look upon. ³And David sent and inquired after the woman. And one said, Is not this Bathsheba, the daughter of Eliam, the wife of Uriah the Hittite? ⁴And David sent messengers, and took her; and she came in unto him, and he lay with her; for she was purified from her uncleanness: and she returned unto her house. ⁵And the woman conceived, and sent and told David, and said, I am with child. ⁶And David sent to Joab, saying, Send me Uriah the Hittite And Joab sent Uriah to David. ⁷And when Uriah was come unto him, David demanded of him how Joab did, and how the people did, and how the war prospered. ⁸And David said to Uriah, Go down to thy house, and wash thy feet. And Uriah departed out of the king's house, and there followed him a mess of meat from the king. ⁹But Uriah slept at the door of the king's house with all the servants of his lord, and went not down to his house. ¹⁰And when they had told David, saying, Uriah went not down unto his house, David said unto Uriah, Camest thou not from thy journey? why then didst thou not go down unto thine house? ¹¹And Uriah said unto David, The ark, and Israel, and Judah, abide in tents; and my lord Joab, and the servants of my lord, are encamped in the open fields; shall I then go drink, and to lie with my wife? as thou livest, and as thy soul liveth, I will not do this thing. ¹²And David said to Uriah, Tarry here today also, and tomorrow I will let thee depart. So Uriah abode in Jerusalem that day, and the morrow.

And when she had brought them unto him to eat, he took hold of her, and said unto her, Come lie me, my sister. [12]And she answered him, Nay, my brother, do not force me; for no such thing ougt to be done in Israel: do not thou this folly. [13]And I, whither shall I cause my shame to go? and as for thee, thou shalt be as one of the fools in Israel. Now therefore, I pray thee, speak unto the king; for he will not withhold me from thee. [14]Howbeit he would not hearken unto her voice: but, being stronger than she, forced her, and lay with her. [15]Then Amnon hated her exceedingly; so that the hatred wherewith he hated her was greater than the love wherewith he had loved her. And Amnon said unto her, Arise, be gone. [16]And she said unto him, There is no cause: this evil in sending me away is greater than the other that thou didst unto me. But he would not hearken unto her.

[17]Then he called his servant that ministered unto him, and said, Put now this woman out from me, and bolt the door after her. [18]And she had a garment of such robes were the king's daughters that were virgins apparelled. Then his servant brought her out, and bolted the door after her. [19]And Tamar put ashes on her head, and rent her garment of diverse colors that was on her, and laid her hand on her head, and went on crying. [20]And Absalom her brother said unto her, Hath Amnon thy brother been with thee? but hold now thy peace, my sister: he is thy brother; regard not this thing. So Tamar remained desolate in her brother Absalom's house.

ow Absalom had com-
manded his servants,
saying, Mark ye now
when Amnon's heart is
merry with wine, and
when I say unto you,
Smite Amnon; then kill
him, fear not: have not I commanded you? be
courageous, and be valiant. [29]And the servants
of Absalom did unto Amnon as Absalom had
commanded. Then all the king's sons arose,
and every man gat him up upon his mule, and
fled. [30]And it came to pass, while they were in
the way, that tidings came to David, saying,
Absalom hath slain all the king's sons, and
there is not one of them left. [31]Then the
king arose, and tare his garments, and lay on
the earth; and all his servants stood by with
their clothes rent. [32]And Jonadab, the son of
Shimeah David's brother, answered and said,
Let not my lord suppose that they have slain all
the young men the king's sons; for by the
appointment of Absalom this hath been determined from the day that he forced his
sister Tamar. [33]Now therefore let not my lord
the king take the thing to his heart, to think
that all the king's sons are dead: for Amnon
only is dead.

nd Absalom met the servants of David. And Absalom rode upon a mule, and the mule went under the thick boughs of a great oak, and his head caught hold of the oak, and he was taken up between the heaven and the earth; and the mule that was under him went away. [10]And a certain man saw it, and told Joab, and said, Behold, I saw Absalom hanged in an oak. [11]And Joab said unto the man that told him, And, behold, thou sawest him, and why didst thou not smite him there to the ground? And I would have given thee ten shekels of silver, and a girdle. [12]And the man said unto Joab, Though I should receive a thousand shekels of silver in mine hand, yet would I not put forth mine hand against the king's son: for in our hearing the king charged thee and Abishai and Ittai, saying, Beware that none touch the young man Absalom. [13]Otherwise I should have wrought falsehood against mine own life: for there is no matter hid from the king, and thou thyself wouldest have set thyself against me. [14]Then said Joab, I may not tarry thus with thee. And he took three darts in his hand, and thrust them through the heart of Absalom, while he was yet alive in the midst of the oak. [15]And ten young men that bare Joab's armor compassed about and smote Absalom, and slew him.

hen he was removed out of the highway, all the people went on after Joab, to pursue after Sheba the son of Bichri. ¹⁴And he went through all the tribes of Israel unto Abel, and to Bethmaachah, and all the Berites: and they were gathered together, and went also after him. ¹⁵And they came and besieged him in Abel of Bethmaachah, and they cast up a bank against the city, and it stood in the trench: and all the people that were with Joab battered the wall, to throw it down. ¹⁶Then cried a wise woman out of the city, Hear, hear; say, I pray you, unto Joab, Come near hither, that I may speak with thee. ¹⁷And when he was come near unto her, the woman said, Art thou Joab? And he answered, I am he. Then she said unto him, Hear the words of thine handmaid. And he answered, I do hear. ¹⁸Then she spake, saying, They were wont to speak in old time, saying, They shall surely ask counsel at Abel: and so they ended the matter. ¹⁹I am one of them that are peaceable and faithful in Israel: why wilt thou swallow up the inheritance of the LORD? ²⁰And Joab answered and said, Far be it, far be it from me, that I should swallow up or destroy. ²¹The matter is not so: but a man of mount Ephraim, Sheba the son of Bichri by name, hath lifted up his hand against the king, even against David: deliver him only, and I will depart from the city. And the woman said unto Joab, Behold, his head shall be thrown to thee over the wall. ²²Then the woman went unto all the people in her wisdom. And they cut off the head of Sheba the son of Bichri, and cast it out to Joab. And he blew a trumpet, and they retired from the city, every man to his tent. And Joab returned to Jerusalem unto the king.

nd this woman's child died in the night; because she overlaid it. [20]And she arose at midnight, and took my son form beside me, while thine handmaid slept, and laid it in her bosom, and laid her dead child in my bosom. [21]And when I rose in the morning to give my child suck, behold, it was dead: but when I had considered it in the morning, behold, it was not my son, which I did bear. [22]And the other woman said, Nay; but the living is my son, and the dead is thy son. And this said, No; but the dead is thy son, and the living is my son. Thus they spake before the king. [23]Then said the king, The one saith, This is my son that liveth, and thy son is the dead: and the other saith, Nay; but thy son is the dead, and my son is the living. [24]And the king said, Bring me a sword. And they brought a sword before the king. [25]And the king said, Divide the living child in two, and give half to the one, and half to the other. [26]Then spake the woman whose the living child was unto the king, for her bowels yearned upon her son, and she said, O my lord, give her the living child, and in no wise slay it. But the other said, Let it be neither mine nor thine, but divide it. [27]Then the king answered and said, Give her the living child, and in no wise slay it: she is the mother therof. [28]And all Israel heard of the judgment which the king had judged; and they feared the king: for they saw that the wisdom of God was in him, to do judgment.

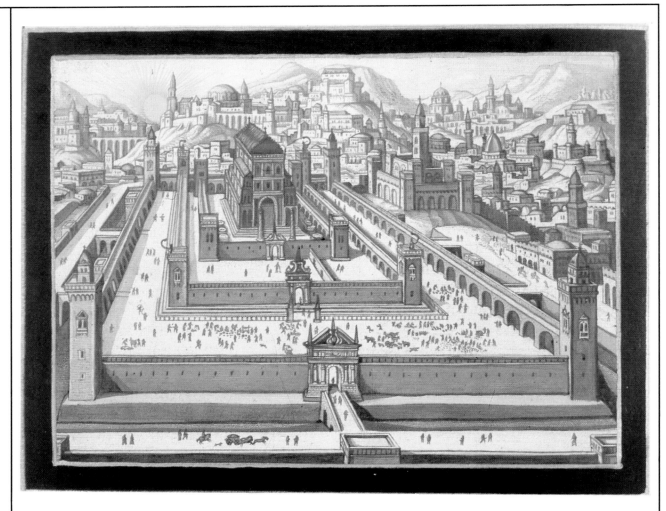

nd he set the cherubims within the inner house: and they stretched forth the wings of the cherubims, so that the wing of the one touched the one wall, and the wing of the other cherub touched the other wall; and their wings touched one another in the midst of the house. ²⁸And he overlaid the cherubims with gold. ²⁹And he carved all the walls of the house round about with carved figures of cherubims and palm trees and open flowers, within and without. ³⁰And the floor of the house he overlaid with gold, within and without. ³¹And for the entering of the oracle he made doors of olive tree; the lintel and side posts were a fifth part of the wall. ³²The two doors also were of olive tree; and he carved upon them carvings of cherumbims and palm trees and open flowers, and overlaid them with gold, and spread gold upon the cherubims, and upon the palm trees. ³³So also made

he for the door of the temple posts of olive tree, a fourth part of the wall. ³⁴And the two doors were of fir tree: the two leaves of the one door were folding, and the two leaves of the other door were folding. ³⁵And he carved thereon cherubims and palm trees and open flowers: and covered them with gold fitted upon the carved work. ³⁶And he built the inner court with three rows of hewed stone, and a row of cedar beams. ³⁷In the fourth year was the foundation of the house of the L<small>ORD</small> laid, in the month Zif: ³⁸And in the eleventh year, in the month Bul, which is the eighth month, was the house finished throughout all the parts thereof, and according to all the fashion of it. So was he seven years in building it.

nd Solomon stood before the altar of the LORD in the presence of all the congregation of Israel, and spread forth his hands toward heaven: [23]And he said, LORD God of Israel, there is no God like thee, in heaven above, or on earth beneath, who keepest covenant and mercy with thy servants that walk before thee with all their heart: [24]Who hast kept with thy servant David my father that thou promisedst him: thou spakest also with thy mouth, and hast fulfilled it with thine hand, as it is this day. [25]Therefore now, LORD God of Israel, keep with thy servant David my father that thou promisedst him, saying, There shall not fail thee a man in my sight to sit on the throne of Israel; so that thy children take heed to their way, that they walk before me as thou hast walked before me. [26]And now, O God of Israel, let thy word, I pray thee, be verified, which thou spakest unto thy servant David my father. [27]But will God indeed dwell on the earth? behold, the heaven and heaven of heavens cannot contain thee; how much less this house that I have builded? [28]Yet have thou respect unto the prayer of thy servant, and to his supplication, O LORD my God, to hearken unto the cry and to the prayer, which thy servant prayeth before thee today: [29]That thine eyes may be open toward this house night and day, even toward the place of which thou hast said, My name shall be there: that thou mayest hearken unto the prayer which thy servant shall make toward this place. [30]And hearken thou to the supplication of thy servant, and of thy people Israel, when they shall pray toward this place: and hear thou in heaven thy dwelling place: and when thou hearest, forgive.

**A**nd when the queen of Sheba heard of the fame of Solomon concerning the name of the LORD, she came to prove him with hard questions. ²And she came to Jerusalem with a very great train, with camels that bare spices, and very much gold, and precious stones: and when she was come to Solomon, she communed with him of all that was in her heart. ³And Solomon told her all her questions: there was not any thing hid from the king, which he told her not. ⁴And when the queen of Sheba had seen all Solomon's wisdom, and the house that he had built, ⁵And the meat of his table, and the sitting of his servants, and the attendance of his ministers, and their apparel, and his cupbearers, and his ascent by which he went up unto the house of the LORD; there was no more spirit in her. ⁶And she said to the king, It was a true report that I heard in mine own land of thy acts and of thy wisdom. ⁷Howbeit I believed not the words, until I came, and mine eyes had seen it: and, behold, the half was not told me: thy wisdom and prosperity exceedeth the fame which I heard. ⁸Happy are thy men, happy are these thy servants, which stand continually before thee, and that hear thy wisdom. ⁹Blessed be the LORD thy God, which delighted in thee, to set thee on the throne of Israel: because the LORD loved Israel for ever, therefore made he thee king, to do judgment and justice. ¹⁰And she gave the king a hundred and twenty talents of gold, and of spices very great store, and precious stones: there came no more such abundance of spices as these which the queen of Sheba gave to king Solomon.

nd it came to pass, as they sat at the table, that the word of the LORD caame unto the prophet that brought him back: [21]And he cried unto the man of God that came from Judah, saying, Thus saith the LORD, Forasmuch as thou hast disobeyed the mouth of the LORD, and hast not kept the commandment which the LORD thy God commanded thee, [22]But camest back, and hast eaten bread and drunk water in the place, of the which the LORD did say to thee, Eat no bread, and drink no water; thy carcass shall not come unto the sepulchre of thy fathers. [23]And it came to pass, after he had eaten bread, and after he had drunk, that he daddled for him the ass, to wit, for the prophet whom he had brought back. [24]And when he was gone, a lion met him by the way, and slew him: and his carcass was cast in the way, and the ass stood by it, the lion also stood by the carcass.

[25]And, behold, men passed by, and saw the carcass cast in the way, and the lion standing by the carcass: and they came and told it in the city where the old prophet dwelt.

n the twenty and seventh year of Asa king of Judah did Zimri reign seven days in Tirzah. And the people were encamped against Gibbethon, which belonged to the Philistines. [16]And the people that were encamped heard say, Zimri hath conspired, and hath also slain the king: wherefore all Israel made Omri, the captain of the host, king over Israel that day in the camp. [17]And Omri went up from Gibbethon, and all Israel with him, and they besieged Tirzah. [18]And it came to pass, when Zimri saw that the city was taken, that he went into the palace of the king's house, and burnt the king's house over him with fire, and died. [19]For his sins which he sinned in doing evil in the sight of the LORD, in walking in the way of Jeroboam, and in his sin which he did, to make Israel to sin.

nd Elijah the Tishbite, who was of the inhabitants of Gilead, said unto Ahab, As the Lord God of Israel liveth, before whom I stand, there shall not be dew nor rain these years, but according to my word. [2]And the word of the Lord came unto him, saying, [3]Get thee hence, and turn thee eastward and hide thyself by the brook Cherith, that is before Jordan. [4]And it shall be, that thou shalt drink of the brook; and I have commanded the ravens to feed thee there. [5]So he went and did according unto the word of the Lord: for he went and dwelt by the brook Cherith, that is before Jordan. [6]And the ravens brought him bread and flesh in the morning, and bread and flesh in the evening; and he drank of the brook. [7]And it came to pass after a while, that the brook dried up, because there had been no rain in the land. [8]And the word of the Lord came unto him,

saying, [9]Arise, get thee to Zarephath, which belongeth to Zidon, and dwell there: behold, I have commanded a widow woman there to sustain thee. [10]So he arose and went to Zarephath. And when he came to the gate of the city, behold, the widow woman was there gathering of sticks: and he called to her, and said, Fetch me, I pray thee, a little water in a vessel, that I may drink.

nd Elijah said unto all the people, Come near unto me. And all the people came near unto him. And he repaired the altar of the LORD that was broken down. [31]And Elijah took twelve stones, according to the number of the tribes of the sons of Jacob, unto whom the word of the LORD came, saying, Israel shall be thy name: [32]And with the stones he built an altar in the name of the LORD: and he made a trench about the altar, as great as would contain two measures of seed. [33]And he put the wood in order, and cut the bullock in pieces, and laid him on the wood, and said, Fill four barrels with water, and pour it on the burnt sacrifice, and on the wood. [34]And he said, Do it the second time. And they did it the second time. And he said, Do it the third time. And they did it the third time. [35]And the water ran round the altar; and he filled the trench also with water. [36]And it came

to pass at the time of the offering of the evening sacrifice, that Elijah the prophet came near, and said, LORD God of Abraham, Isaac, and of Israel, let it be known this day that thou art God in Israel, and that I am thy servant, and that I have done all these things at thy word. [37]Hear me, O LORD, hear me, that this people may know that thou art the LORD God, and that thou hast turned their heart back again. [38]Then the fire of the LORD fell, and consumed the burnt sacrifice, and the wood, and the stones, and the dust, and licked up the water that was in the trench. [39]And when all the people saw it, they fell on their faces: and they said, The LORD, he is the God; the LORD, he is the God. [40]And Elijah said unto them, Take the prophets of Baal; let not one of them escape. And they took them: and Elijah brought them down to the brook Kishon, and slew them there.

nd Ahab told Jezebel all that Elijah had done, and withal how he had slain all the prophets with the sword. [2]Then Jezebel sent a messenger unto Elijah, saying, So let the gods do to me, and more also, if I make not thy life as the life of one of them by tomorrow about this time. [3]And when he saw that, he arose, and went for his life, and came to Beersheba, which belongeth to Judah, and left his servant there. [4]But he himself went a day's journey into the wilderness, and came and sat down under a juniper tree: and he requested for himself that he might die; and said, It is enough; now, O LORD, take away my life; for I am not better than my fathers. [5]And as he lay and slept under a juniper tree, behold, then an angel touched him, and said unto him, Arise and eat. [6]And he looked, and, behold, there was a cake baken on the coals, and a cruse of water at his head. And he did eat and drink, and laid him down again. [7]And the angel of the LORD came again the second time, and touched him, and said, Arise and eat; because the journey is too great for thee. [8]And he arose, and did eat and drink, and went in the strength of that meat forty days and forty nights unto Horeb the mount of God. [9]And he came thither unto a cave, and lodged there; and, behold, the word of the LORD came to him, and he said unto him, What doest thou here, Elijah?

o the king of Israel and Jehoshaphat the king of Judah went up to Ramoth-gilead. [30]And the king of Israel said unto Jehoshaphat, I will disguise myself, and enter into the battle; but put thou on thy robes. And the king of Israel disguised himself, and went into the battle. [31]But the king of Syria commanded his thirty and two captains that had rule over his chariots, saying, Fight neither with small nor great, save only with the king of Israel. [32]And it came to pass, when the captains of the chariots saw Jehoshaphat, that they said, Surely it is the king of Israel. And they turned aside to fight against him: and Jehoshaphat cried out. [33]And it came to pass, when the captains of the chariots perceived that it was not the king of Israel, that they turned back from pursuing him. [34]And a certain man drew a bow at a venture, and smote the king of Israel between the joints of the harness: wherefore he said unto the driver of his chariot, Turn thine hand, and carry me out of the host; for I am wounded. [35]And the battle increased that day: and the king was stayed up in his chariot against the Syrians, and died at even: and the blood ran out of the wound into the midst of the chariots. [36]And there went a proclamation throughout the host about the going down of the sun, saying, Every man to his city, and every man to his own country. [37]So the king died, and was brought to Samaria; and they buried the king in Samaria. [38]And one washed the chariot in the pool of Samaria; and the dogs licked up his blood; and they washed his armor; according unto the word of the Lord which he spake.

nd Elijah said unto him, Elisha, tarry here, I pray thee; for the LORD hath sent me to Jericho. And he said, As the LORD liveth, and as thy soul liveth, I will not leave thee. So they came to Jericho. ⁵And the sons of the prophets that were at Jericho came to Elisha, and said unto him, Knowest thou that the LORD will take away thy master from thy head today? And he answered, Yea, I know it; hold ye your peace. ⁶And Elijah said unto him, Tarry, I pray thee, here; for the LORD hath sent me to Jordan. And he said, As the LORD liveth, and as thy soul liveth, I will not leave thee. And they two went on. ⁷And fifty men of the sons of the prophets went, and stood to view afar off: and they two stood by Jordan. ⁸And Elijah took his mantle, and wrapped it together, and smote the waters, and they were divided hither and thither, so that they two went over on dry ground. ⁹And it came to pass, when they were gone over, that Elijah said unto Elisha, Ask what I shall do for thee, before I be taken away from thee. And Elisha said, I pray thee, let a double portion of thy spirit be upon me. ¹⁰And he said, Thou hast asked a hard thing: nevertheless, if thou see me when I am taken from thee, it shall be so unto thee; but if not, it shall not be so. ¹¹And it came to pass, as they still went on, and talked, that, behold, there appeared a chariot of fire, and horses of fire, and parted them both asunder; and Elijah went up by a whirl-wind into heaven.

nd he went up from thence unto Beth-el: and as he was going up by the way, there came forth little children out of the city, and mocked him, and said unto him, Go up, thou bald head; go up, thou bald head. ¹²⁴And he turned back, and looked on them, and cursed them in the name of the Lᴏʀᴅ. And there came forth two she bears out of the wood, and tare forty and two children of them. ²⁵And he went from thence to mount Carmel, and from thence he returned to Samaria.

ow there cried a certain woman of the wives of the sons of the prophets unto Elisha, saying, Thy servant my husband is dead; and thou knowest that thy servant did fear the LORD: and the creditor is come to take unto him my two sons to be bondmen. ²And Elisha said unto her, What shall I do for thee? tell me, what hast thou in the house? And she said, Thine handmaid hath not any thing in the house, save a pot of oil. ³Then he said, Go, borrow thee vessels abroad of all thy neighbors, even empty vessels; borrow not a few. ⁴And when thou art come in, thou shalt shut the door upon thee and upon thy sons, and shalt pour out into all those vessels, and thou shalt set aside that which is full. ⁵So she went from him, and shut the door upon her and upon her sons, who brought the vessels to her; and she poured out. ⁶And it came to pass, when the vessels were full, that she said unto her son, Bring me yet a vessel. And he said unto her, There is not a vessel more. And the oil stayed. ⁷Then she came and told the man of God. And he said, Go, sell the oil, and pay thy debt, and live thou and thy children of the rest.

And it was so, when Elisha the man of God had heard that the king of Israel had rent his clothes, that he sent to the king, saying, Wherefore hast thou rent thy clothes? let him come now to me, and he shall know that there is a prophet in Israel. [9]So Naaman came with his horses and with his chariot, and stood at the door of the house of Elisha. [10]And Elisha sent a messenger unto him, saying, Go and wash in Jordan seven times, and thy flesh shall come again to thee, and thou shalt be clean. [11]But Naaman was wroth, and went away, and said, Behold, I thought, He will surely come out to me, and stand, and call on the name of the Lord his God, and strike his hand over the place, and recover the leper. [12]Are not Abana and Pharpar, rivers of Damascus, better than all the waters of Israel? may I not wash in them, and be clean? So he turned and went away in a rage.

[13]And his servants came near, and spake unto him, and said, My father, if the prophet had bid thee do some great thing, wouldest thou not have done it? how much rather then, when he saith to thee, Wash, and be clean? [14]Then went he down, and dipped himself seven times in Jordan, according to the saying of the man of God: and his flesh came again like unto the flesh of a little child, and he was clean.

nd when the servant of the man of God was risen early, and gone forth, behold, a host compassed the city both with horses and chariots. And his servant said unto him, Alas, my master! how shall we do? ¹⁶And he answered, Fear not: for they that be with us are more than they that be with them. ¹⁷And Elisha prayed, and said, LORD, I pray thee, open his eyes, that he may see. And the LORD opened the eyes of the young man; and he saw: and, behold, the mountain was full of horses and chariots of fire round about Elisha. ¹⁸And when they came down to him, Elisha prayed unto the LORD, and said, Smite this people, I pray thee, with blindness. And he smote them with blindness according to the word of Elisha. ¹⁹And Elisha said unto them, This is not the way, neither is this the city: follow me, and I will bring you to the man whom ye seek. But he led them to Samaria. ²⁰And it came to pass, when they were come into Samaria, that Elisha said, LORD, open the eyes of these men, that they may see. And the LORD opened their eyes, and they saw; and, behold, they were in the midst of Samaria. ²¹And the king of Israel said unto Elisha, when he saw them, My father, shall I smite them? shall I smite them? ²²And he answered, Thou shalt not smite them: wouldest thou smite those whom thou hast taken captive with thy sword and with thy bow? set bread and water before them, that they may eat and drink, and go to their master. ²³And he prepared great provision for them: and when they had eaten and drunk, he sent them away, and they went to their master. So the bands of Syria came no more into the land of Israel.

nd the king appointed the lord on whose hand he leaned to have the charge of the gate: and the people trode upon him in the gate, and he died, as the man of God had said, who spake when the king came down to him. [18]And it came to pass as the man of God had spoken to the king, saying, Two measures of barley for a shekel, and a measure of fine flour for a shekel, shall be tomorrow about this time in the gate of Samaria: [19]And the lord answered the man of God, and said, Now, behold, if the Lord should make windows in heaven, might such a thing be? And he said, Behold, thou shalt see it with thine eyes, but shalt not eat thereof. [20]And so it fell out unto him: for the people trode upon him in the gate, and he died.

nd when Jehu was come to Jezreel, Jeze-bel heard of it; and she painted her face, and tired her head, and looked out at a window. ³¹And as Jehu entered in at the gate, she said, had Zimri peace, who slew his master? ³²And he lifted up his face to the window, and said, Who is on my side? who? And there looked out to him two or three eunuchs. ³³And he said, Throw her down. So they threw her down: and some of her blood was sprinkled on the wall, and on the horses; and he trode her under foot. ³⁴And when he was come in, he did eat and drink, and said, Go, see now this cursed woman, and bury her: for she is a king's daughter. ³⁵And they went to bury her: but they found no more of her than the skull, and the feet, and the palms of her hands. ³⁶Wherefore they came again, and told him. And he said, This is the word of the Lord, which he spake by his servant Elijah the Tishbite, saying, In the portion of Jezreel shall dogs eat the flesh of Jezebel: ³⁷And the carcass of Jezebel shall be as dung upon the face of the field in the portion of Jezreel; so that they shall not say, This is Jezebel.

nd Elisha died, and they buried him. And the bands of the Moabites invaded the land at the coming in of the year. [21]And it came to pass, as they were burying a man, that, behold, they spied a band of men; and they cast the man into the sepulchre of Elisha: and when the man was let down, and touched the bones of Elisha, he revived, and stood up on his feet.

ow it came to pass in the third year of Hoshea son of Elah king of Israel, that Hezekiah the son of Ahaz king of Judah began ro reign. ²Twenty and five years old was he when he began to reign; and he reigned twenty and nine years in Jerusalem. His mother's name also was Abi, the daughter of Zachariah. ³And he did that which was right in the sight of the LORD, according to all that David his father did. ⁴He removed the high places, and brake the images, and cut down the groves, and brake in pieces the brasen serpent that Moses had made: for unto those days the children of Israel did burn incense to it: and he called it Nehushtan. ⁵He trusted in the LORD God of Israel; so that after him was none like him among all the kings of Judah, nor any that were before him. ⁶For he clave to the LORD, and departed not from following him, but kept his commandments, which the

LORD commanded Moses. ⁷And the LORD was with him; and he prospered whithersoever he went forth: and he rebelled against the king of Assyria, and served him not. ⁸He smote the Philistines, even unto Gaza, and the borders thereof, from the tower of the watchmen to the fenced city.

or out of Jerusalem shall go forth a remnant, and they that escape our of mount Zion: the zeal of the Lord of hosts shall do this. ³²Therefore thus saith the Lord concerning the king of Assyria, He shall not come into this city, nor shoot an arrow there, nor cast a bank against it. ³³By the way that he came, by the same shall he return, and shall not come into this city, saith the Lord. ³⁴For I will defend this city, to save it, for mine own shake, and for my servant David's sake. ³⁵And it came to pass that night, that the angel of the Lord went out, and smote in the camp of the Assyrians and hundred fourscore and five thousand: and when they arose early in the morning, behold, they were all dead corpses. ³⁶So Sennacherib king of Assyria departed, and went and returned, and dwelt at Nineveh. ³⁷And it came to pass, as he was worshipping in the house of Nisroch his god, that Adram-melech and Sharezer his sons smote him with the sword: and they escaped into the land of Armenia. And Esarhaddon his son reigned in his stead.

n those days was Hezekiah sick unto death. And the prophet Isaiah the son of Amoz came to him, and said unto him, Thus saith the LORD, Set thine house in order; for thou shalt die, and not live. [2]Then he turned his face to the wall, and prayed unto the LORD, saying, [3]I beseech thee, O LORD, remember now how I have walked before thee in truth and with a perfect heart, and have done that which is good in thy sight. And Hezekiah wept sore. [4]And it came to pass, afore Isaiah was gone out into the middle court, that the word of the LORD came to him, saying, [5]Turn again, and tell Hezekiah, the captain of my people, Thus saith the LORD, the God of David thy father, I have heard thy prayer, I have seen thy tears: behold, I will heal thee: on the third day thou shalt go up unto the house of the LORD. [6]And I will add unto thy days fifteen years; and I will deliver thee and this city out of the hand of the king of Assyria; and I will defend this city for mine own sake, and for my servant David's sake. [7]And Isaiah said, Take a lump of figs. And they took and laid it on the boil, and he recovered.

nd the king command-
ed all the people, say-
ing, Keep the passover
unto the Lord your
God, as it is written in
the book of this cove-
nant. ²²Surely there
was not holden such a passover from the days
of the judges that judged Israel, nor in all the
days of the kings of Israel, nor of the kings of
Judah; ²³But in the eighteenth year of king Josiah, wherein this passover was holden to the
Lord in Jerusalem. ²⁴Moreover the workers
with familiar spirits, and the wizards, and the
images, and the idols, and all the abominations
that were spied in the land of Judah and in
Jerusalem, did Josiah put away, that he might
perform the words of the law which were
written in the book that Hilkiah the priest
found in the house of the Lord. ²⁵And like
unto him was there no king before him, that
turned to the Lord with all his heart, and with
all his soul, and with all his might, according to
all the law of Moses; neither after him arose
there any like him. ²⁶Notwithstanding the
Lord turned not from the fierceness of his
great wrath, wherewith his anger was kindled
against Judah, because of all the provoca-
tions that Manasseh had provoked him withal.
²⁷And the Lord said, I will remove Judah also
out of my sight, as I have removed Israel, and
will cast off this city Jerusalem which I have
chosen, and the house of which I said, My
name shall be there. ²⁸Now the rest of the acts
of Josiah, and all that he did, are they not
written in the book of the chronicles of the
kings of Judah?

**A**nd it came to pass in the ninth year of his reign, in the tenth month, in the tenth day of the month, that Nebuchadnezzar king of Babylon came, he, and all his host, against Jerusalem, and pitched against it: and they built forts against it round about. [2]And the city was besieged unto the eleventh year of king Zedekiah. [3]And on the ninth day of the fourth month the famine prevailed in the city, and there was no bread for the people of the land. [4]And the city was broken up, and all the men of war fled by night by the way of the gate between two walls, which is by the king's garden: (now the Chaldees were against the city round about:) and the king went the way toward the plain. [5]And the army of the Chaldees persued after the king, and overtook him in the plains of Jericho: and all his army were scattered from him. [6]So they took the king, and brought him up to the king of Babylon to Riblah; and they gave judgment upon him. [7]And they slew the sons of Zedekiah before his eyes, and put out the eyes of Zedekiah, and bound him with fetters of brass, and carried him to Babylon.

And David lifted up his eyes and saw the angel of the LORD stand between the earth and the heaven, having a drawn sword in his hand stretched out over Jerusalem. Then David and the elders of Israel, who were clothed in sackcloth, fell upon their faces. [17]And David said unto God, Is it not I that commanded the people to be numbered? even I it is that have sinned and done evil indeed; but as for these sheep, what have they done? let thine hand, I pray thee, O LORD my God, be on me, and on my father's house; but not on thy people, that they should be plagued. [18]Then the angel of the LORD commanded Gad to say to David, that David should go up, and set up an altar unto the LORD in the threshingfloor of Oranan the Jebusite. [19]And David went up at the saying of Gad, which he spake in the name of the LORD.

And Jehoshaphat bowed his head with his face to the ground: and all Judah and the inhabitants of Jerusalem fell before the LORD, worsh-ipping the LORD. ¹⁹And the Levites, of the children of the Kohathites, and of the children of the Korhites, stood up to praise the LORD God of Israel with a loud voice on high. ²⁰And they rose early in the morning, and went forth into the wilderness of Tekoa: and as they went forth, Jehoshaphat stood and said, Hear me, O Judah, and ye inhabitants of Jerusalem; Believe in the LORD your God, so shall ye be established; believe his prophets, so shall ye prosper. ²¹And when he had consulted with the people, he appointed singers unto the LORD, and that should praise the beauty of holiness, as they went out before the army, and to say, Praise the LORD; for his mercy endureth for ever. ²²And when they began to sing and to praise, the LORD set ambushments against the children of Ammon, Moab, and mount Seir, which were come against Judah; and they were smitten.

ow after the death of Jehoiada came the princes of Judah, and made obeisance to the king. Then the king hearkened unto them. [18]And they left the house of the LORD God of their fathers, and served groves and idols: and wrath came upon Judah and Jerusalem for this their trespass. [19]Yet he sent prophets to them, to bring them again unto the LORD; and they testified against them; but they would not give ear. [20]And the spirit of God came upon Zechariah the son of Jehoiada the priest, which stood above the people, and said unto them, Thus saith God, Why transgress ye the commandments of the LORD, that ye cannot prosper? because ye have forsaken the LORD, he hath also forsaken you. [21]And they conspired against him, and stoned him with stones at the commandment of the king in the court of the house of the LORD. [22]Thus Joash the king remembered not the kindness which Jehoiada his father had done to him, but slew his son. And when he died, he said, The LORD look upon it, and require it.

hen Eliashib the high priest rose up with his brethren the priests, and they builded the sheep gate; they sanctified it, and set up the doors of it; even unto the tower of Meah they sanctified it, unto the tower of Hananeel. [2]And next unto him builded the men of Jericho. And next to them builded Zaccur the son of Imri. [3]But the fish gate did the sons of Hassenaah build, who also laid the beams thereof, and set up the doors thereof, the locks thereof, and the bars thereof. [4]And next unto them repaired Meremoth the son of Urijah, the son of Koz. And next unto them repaired Meshullam the son of Berechiah, the son of Meshezabeel. And next unto them repaired Zadok the son of Baana. [5]And next unto them the Tekoites repaired; but their nobles put not their necks to the work of their LORD. [6]Morevoer the old gate repaired Jehoiada the son of Paseah, and Meshullam

the son of Besodeiah; they laid the beams thereof, and set up the doors thereof, and the locks thereof, and the bars thereof. [7]And next unto them repaired Melatiah the Gibeonite, and Jadon the Meronothite, the men of Gibeon, and of Mezpah, unto the throne of the governor on this side the river. [8]Next unto him repaired Uzziel the son of Harhaiah, of the goldsmiths. Next unto him also repaired Hananiah the son of one of the apothecaries, and they fortified Jerusalem unto the broad wall. [9]And next unto them repaired Rephaiah the son of Hur, the ruler of the half part of Jerusalem. [10]And next unto them repaired Jedaiah the son of Harumaph, even over against his house. And next unto him repaired Hattush the son of Hashabniah. [11]Malchijah the son of Harim, and Hashub the son of Pahathmoab, repaired the other piece, and the tower of the furnaces. [12]And next unto him repaired Shallum the son of Halohesh, the ruler of the half part of Jerusalem, he and his daughter.

I n that night could not the king sleep, and he commanded to bring the book of records of the chronicles; and they were read before the king. ²And it was found written, that Mordecai had told of Bigthana and Teresh, two of the king's chamberlains, the keepers of the door, who sought to lay hand on the king Ahasuerus. ³And the king said, What honour and dignity hath been done to Mordecai for this? Then said the king's servants that ministered unto him, There is nothing done for him. ⁴And the king said, Who is in the court? Now Haman was come into the outward court of the king's house, to speak unto the king to hang Mordecai on the gallows that he had prepared for him. ⁵And the king's servants said unto him, Behold, Haman standeth in the court. And the king said, Let him come in. ⁶So Haman came in. And the king said unto him, What shall be done unto the man whom the king delighteth to honor Now Haman thought in his heart, To whom would the king delight to do honor more than to myself? ⁷And Haman answered the king, For the man whom the king delighteth to honor, ⁸Let the royal apparel be brought which the king useth to wear, and the horse that the king rideth upon, and the crown royal which is set upon his head: ⁹And let this apparel and horse be delivered to the hand of one of the king's most noble princes, that they may array the man withal whom the king delighteth to honor, and bring him on horseback through the street of the city, and proclaim before him, Thus shall it be done to the man whom the king delighteth to honor. ¹⁰Then the king said to Haman, Make haste, and take the apparel and the horse, as thou hast said, and do even so to Mordecai the Jew, that sitteth at the king's gate: at morning fail of all that thou hast spoken.

o the king and Haman came to banquet with Esther the queen. [2]And the king said again unto Esther on the second day at the banquet of wine, What is thy petition, queen Esther? and it shall be granted thee: and what is thy request? and it shall be performed, even to the half of the kingdom. [3]Then Esther the queen answered and said, If I have found favor in thy sight, O king, and if it please the king, let my life be given me at my petition, and my people at my request. [4]For we are sold, I and my people, to be destroyed, to be slain, and to perish. But if we had been sold for bondmen and bondwomen, I had held my tongue, although the enemy could not countervail the king's damage. [5]Then the king Ahasuerus answered and said unto Esther the queen, Who is he, and where is he, that durst presume in his heart to do so? [6]And Esther said, The adversary and enemy is this wicked Haman. Then Haman was afraid before the king and the queen. [7]And the king arising from the banquet of wine in his wrath went into the palace garden: and Haman stood up to make request for his life to Esther the queen; for he saw that there was evil determined against him by the king. [8]Then the king returned out of the palace garden into the palace of the banquet of wine; and Haman was fallen upon the bed whereon Esther was. Then said the king, Will he force the queen also before me in the house? As the word went out of the king's mouth, they covered Haman's face. [9]And Harbonah, one of the chamberlains, said before the king, Behold also, the gallows fifty cubits high, which Haman had made for Mordecai, who had spoken good for the king, standeth in the house of Haman. Then the king said, Hang him thereon. [10]So they hanged Haman on the gallows that he had prepared for Mordecai. Then was the king's wrath pacified.

nd Satan answered the LORD, and said, Skin for skin, yea, all that a man hath will he give for his life. ⁵But put forth thine hand now, and touch his bone and his flesh, and he will curse thee to thy face. ⁶And the LORD said unto Satan, Behold, he is in thine hand; but save his life. ⁷So went Satan forth from the presence of the LORD, and smote Job with sore boils from the sole of his foot unto his crown. ⁸And he took him a potsherd to scrape himself withal; and he sat down among the ashes. ⁹Then said his wife unto him, Dost thou still retain thine integrity? curse God, and die. ¹⁰But he said unto her, Thou speakest as one of the foolish women speaketh. What? shall we receive good at the hand of God, and shall we not receive evil? In all this did not Job sin his lips. ¹¹Now when Job's three friends heard of all this evil that was come upon him, they came every one from his own place: Eliphaz the Temanite, and Bildad the Shuhite, and Zophar the Naamathite: for they had made an appointment together to come to mourn with him and to comfort him. ¹²And when they lifted up their eyes afar off, and knew him not, they lifted up their voice, and wept; and they rent every one his mantle, and sprinkled dust upon their heads toware heaven. ¹³So they sat down with him upon the ground seven days and seven nights, and none spake a word unto him: for they saw that his grief was very great.

ORD, how are they increased that trouble me! many are they that rise up against me. [2]Many there be which say of my soul, There is no help for him in god. Selah. [3]But thou, O LORD, art a shield for me; my glory, and the lifter up of mine head. [4]I cried unto the LORD with my voice, and he heard me out of his holy hill. Selah. [5]I laid me down and slept; I awaked; for the LORD sustained me. [6]I will not be afraid of ten thousands of people, that have set themselves against me round about. [7]Arise, O LORD; save me, O my God: for thou hast smitten all mine enemies upon the cheek bone; thou hast broken the teeth of the ungodly. [8]Salvation belongeth unto the LORD: thy blessing is upon thy people. Selah.

he song of songs, which is Solomon's. ²Let him kiss me with the kisses of his mouth: for thy love is better than wine. ³Because of the savor of thy good ointments thy name is as ointment poured forth, therefore do the virgins love thee. ⁴Draw me, we will run after thee: the king hath brought me into his chambers: we will be glad and rejoice in thee, we will remember thy love more than wine: the upright love thee. ⁵I am black, but comely, O ye daughters of Jerusalem, as the tents of Kedar, as the curtains of Solomon. ⁶Look not upon me, because I am black, because the sun hath looked upon me: my mother's children were angry with me: they made me the keeper of the vineyards; but mine own vineyard have I not kept. ⁷Tell me, O thou whom my soul loveth, where thou feedest, where thou makest thy flock to rest at noon: for why should I be as one that turneth aside by the flocks of thy companions? ⁸If thou know not, O thou fairest among women, go thy way forth by the footsteps of the flock, and feed thy kids beside the shepherd's tents. ⁹I have compared thee, O my love, to a company of horses in Pharaoh's chariots. ¹⁰Thy cheeks are comely with rows of Jewels, thy neck with chains of gold. ¹¹We will make thee borders of gold with studs of silver. ¹²While the king sitteth at his table, my spikenard sendeth forth the smell thereof. ¹³A bundle of myrrh is my well beloved unto me; he shall lie all night betwixt my breasts. ¹⁴My beloved is unto me as a cluster of camphire in the vineyards of Engedi. ¹⁵Behold, thou art fair, my love; behold, thou art fair; thou hast doves' eyes. ¹⁶Behold, thou art fair, my beloved, yea, pleasant: also our bed is green. ¹⁷The beams of our house are cedar, and our rafters of fir.

n the year that king Uz-
ziah died I saw also the
LORD sitting upon a
throne, high and lifted
up, and his train filled
the temple. ²Above it
stood the serahimp:
each one had sixs wings; with twain he covered
his face, and with twain he covered his feet.
³And one cried unto another, and said, Holy,
holy, holy, is the LORD of hosts: the whole
earth is full of his glory. ⁴And the posts of the
door moved at the voice of him that cried, and
the house was filled with smoke. ⁵Then said I,
Woe is me! for I am undone; because I am a
man of unclean lips, and I dwell in the midst of
a people of unclean lips: for mine eyes have
seen the King, the LORD of hosts. ⁶Then flew
one of the seraphims unto me, having a live
coal in his hand, which he had taken with the
tongs from off the altar: ⁷And he laid it upon
my mouth, and said, Lo, this hath touched thy
lips; and thine iniquity is taken away, and thy

sin purged. ⁸Also I heard the voice of the
LORD, saying, Whom shall I send, and who
will go for us? Then said I, Here am I; send
me. ⁹And he said, Go, and tell this people,
Hear ye indeed, but understand not; and see
ye indeed, but perceive not. ¹⁰Make the heart
of this people fat, and make their ears heavy,
and shut their eyes; lest they see with their
eyes, and hear with their ears, and understand with their heart, and convert, and be
healed. ¹¹Then said I, LORD, how long? And
he answered, Until the cities be wasted without inhabitant, and the houses without man,
and the land be utterly desolate, ¹²And the
LORD have removed men far away, and there
be a great forsaking in the midst of the land.

hen the word of the LORD came unto me, saying, [5]Before I formed thee in the belly, I knew thee; and before thou camest forth out of the womb I sanctified thee, and I ordained thee a prophet unto the nations. [6]Then said I, Ah, LORD God! behold, I cannot speak: for I am a child. [7]But the LORD said unto me, Say not, I am a child: for thou shalt go to all that I shall send thee, and whatsoever I command thee thou shalt speak. [8]Be not afraid of their faces: for I am with thee to deliver thee, saith the LORD. [9]Then the LORD put forth his hand, and touched my mouth. And the LORD said unto me, Behold, I have put my words in thy mouth. [10]See, I have this day set thee over the nations and over the kingdoms, to root out, and to pull down, and to destroy, and to throw down, to build, and to plant. [11]Moreover the word of the LORD came unto me, saying, Jeremiah, what seest thou?

And I said, I see a rod of an almond tree. [12]Then said the LORD unto me, Thou hast well seen: for I will hasten my word to perform it.

hen Shepatiah the son of Mattan, and Gedaliah the son of Pashur, and Jucal the son of Shelemiah, and Pshur the son of Malchiah, heard the words that Jeremiah had spoken unto all the people, saying, [2]Thus saith the LORD, He that remaineth in this city shall die by the sword, by the famine, and by the pestilence: but he that goeth forth to the Chaldeans. shall live, for he shall have his life for a prey, and shall live. [3]Thus saith the LORD, This city shall surely be given into the hand of the king of Babylon's army, which shall take it. [4]Therefore the princes said unto the king, We beseech thee, let this man be put to death: for thus he weakeneth the hands of the men of war that remain in this city, and the hands of all the people, in speaking such words unto them: for this man seeketh not the welfare of this people, but the hurt. [5]Then Zedekiah the king said, Behold, he is in your hand: for the king is not he that can do any thing against you. [6]Then took they Jeremiah, and cast him into the dungeon of Malchiah the sons of Hammelech, that was in the court of the prison: and they let down Jeremiah with cords. And in the dungeon there was no water, but mire: so Jeremiah sunk in the mire.

nd the likeness of the firmament upon the heads of the living creature was as the color of the terrible crystal, stretched forth over their heads above. ²³And under the firmament were their wings straight, the one toward the other: every one had two, which covered on this side and every one had two, which covered on that side, their bodies. ²⁴And when they went, I heard the noise of their wings, like the noise of great waters, as the voice of the Almighty, the voice of speech, as the noise of an host when they stood, they let down their wings. ²⁵And there was a voice from the firmament that was over their heads, when they stood, and had let down their wings. ²⁶And above the firmament that was over their heads was the likeness of a throne, as the appearance of a sapphire stone: and upon the likeness of the throne was the likeness as the appearance of a man above

upon it. ²⁷And I saw as the color of amber, as the appearance of fire round about within it, from the appearance of his loins even upward, and from the appearance of his loins even downward, I saw as it were the appearance of fire, and it had brightness round about. ²⁸As the appearance of the bow that is in the cloud in the day of rain, so was the appearance of the brightness round about. This was the appearance of the likeness of the glory of the LORD. And when I saw it, I fell upon my face, and I heard a voice of one that spake.

nd he said unto me, Son of man, can these bones live? And I answered, O Lord God, Thou knowest. [4]Again he said unto me, Prophesy upon these bones, and say unto them, O ye dry bones, hear the word of the Lord. [5]Thus saith the LordGod unto these bones; Behold, I will cause breath to enter into you, and ye shall live: [6]And I will lay sinews upon you, and will bring up flesh upon you, and cover you with skin, and put breath in you, and ye shall live; and ye shall know that I am the Lord. [7]So I prophesied as I was commanded: and as I prophesied, there was a noise, and behold a shaking, and the bones came together, bone to his bone. [8]And when I beheld, lo, the sinews and the flesh came up upon them, and the skin covered them above: but there was no breath in them. [9]Then said he unto me, Prophesy unto the wind, prophesy, son of man, and say to the wind. Thus saith the Lord God; Come from the four winds, O breath, and breathe upon these slain, that they may live. [10]So I prophesied as he commanded me, and the breath came into them, and they lived, and stood up upon their feet, an exceeding great army. [11]Then he said unto me, Son of man, these bones are the whole house of Israel: behold, they say, Our bones are dried, and our hope is lost: we are cut off for our parts. [12]Therefore prophesy and say unto them, Thus saith the Lord God; Behold, O my people, I will open your graves, and cause you to come up out of your graves, and bring you into the land of Israel.

his is the dream; and we will tell the interpretation thereof before the king. [37]Thou, o king, art a king of kings: for the God of heaven hath given thee a kingdom, power, and strength, and glory. [38]And wheresoever the children of men dwell, the beasts of the field and the fowls of the heaven hath he given into thine hand, and hath made thee ruler over them all. Thou art this head of gold. [39] And after thee shall arise another kingdom inferior to thee, and another third kingdom of brass, which shall bear rule over all the earth. [40]And the fourth kingdom shall be strong as iron: for as much as iron breaketh in pieces and subdueth all things: and as iron that breaketh all these, shall it break in pieces and bruise. [41]And whereas thou sawest the feet and toes, part of potters' clay, and part of iron, the kingdom shall be divided; but there shall be in it of the strength of the iron, for as much as thou sawest the iron mixed with miry clay. [42]And as the toes of the feet were part of iron, and part of clay, so the kingdom shall be partly strong, and partly broken. [43]And whereas thou sawest iron mixed with miry clay, they shall mingle themselves with the seed of men: but they shall not cleave one to another, even as iron is not mixed with clay. [44]And in the days of these kings shall the God of heaven set up a kingdom, which shall never be destroyed: and the kingdom shall not be left to other people, but it shall break in pieces and consume all these kingdoms, and it shall stand for ever.

hen was Nebuchadnez-zar full of fury, and the form of his visage was changed against Shadrach, Meshach, and Abednego: therefore he spake, and commanded that they should heat the furnace one seven times more that it was wont to be heated. ²⁰And he commanded the most mighty men that were in his army to bind Shadrach, Meshach, and Abednego, and to cast them into the burning fiery furnace. ²¹Then these men were bound in their coats, their hosen, and their hats, and their other garments, and were cast into the midst of the burning fiery furnace. ²²Therefore because the king's commandment was urgent, and the furnace exceeding hot, the flame of the fire slew those men that took up Shadrach, Meshach, and Abednego. ²³And these three men, Shadrach, Meshach, and Abednego, fell down bound into the midst of the burning fiery furnace.

elshazzar the king made a great feast to a thousand of his lords, and drank wine before the thousand . [2]Belshazzar, whiles he tasted the wine, commanded to bring the golden and silver vessels which his father Nebuchadnezzar had taken out of the temple which was in Jerusalem; that the king, and his princes, his wives, and his concubines, might drink therein. [3]Then they brought the golden vessels that were taken out of the temple of the house of God which was at Jerusalem; and the king, and his princes, his wives, and his concubines, drank in them. [4]They drank wine, and praised the gods of gold, and of silver, of brass, of iron, of wook, and of stone. [5]In the same hour came forth fingers of a man's hand, and wrote over against the candlestick upon the plaster of the wall of the king's palace: and the king saw the part of the hand that wrote. [6]Then the king's countenance was changed, and his thoughts troubled him, so that the joints of his loins were loosed, and his knees smote one against another. [7]The king cried aloud to bring in the astrologers, the Chaldeans, and the soothsayers. And the kings spake, and said to the wise men of Babylon, Whosoever shall read this writing, and shew me the interpretation thereof, shall be clothed with scarlet, and have a chain of gold about his neck, and shall be the third ruler in the kingdom.

Then these men assembled, and found Daniel praying and making supplication before his God. [12]Then they came near, and spake before the king concerning the king's decree; Hast thou not signed a decree, that every man that shall ask a petition of any God or man within thirty days, save of thee, o king, shall be cast into the den of lions? The king answered and said, The thing is true, according to the law of the Medes and Persians, which altereth not. [13]Then answered they and said before the king, That Daniel, which is of the children of the captivity of Judah, regardeth not thee, O king, nor the decree that thou hast signed, but maketh his petition three times a day, [14]Then the king, when he heard these words, was sore displeased with himself, and set his heart on Daniel to deliver him: and he labored till the going down of the sun to deliver him. [15]Then these men assembled unto the king, and said unto the king, Know, O king, that the law of the Medes and Persians is, That no decree nor statute which the king establisheth may be changed. [16]Then the king commanded, and they brought Daniel, and cast him into the den of lions. Now the king spake and said unto Daniel, Thy God whom thou servest continually, he will deliver thee. [17]And a stone was brought, and laid upon the mouth of the den; and the king sealed it with his own signet, and with the signet of his lords; that the purpose might not be changed concerning Daniel. [18]Then the king went to his palace, and passed the night fasting: neither were instruments of music brought before him: and his sleep went from him. [19]Then the king arose very early in the morning, and went in haste unto the den of lions.

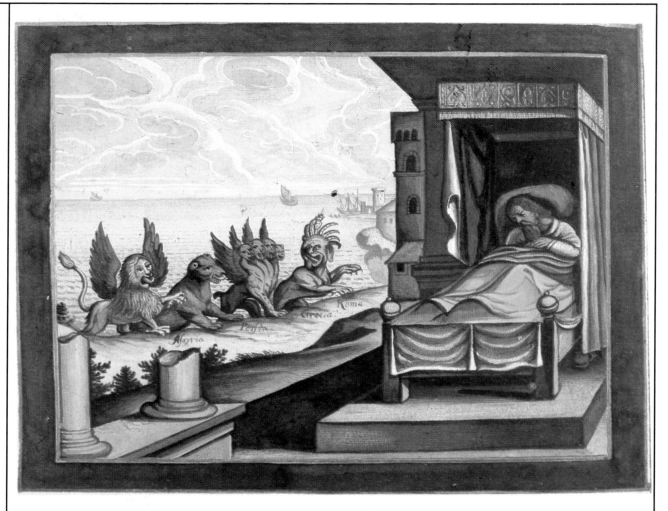

n the first year of Belshazzar king of Babylon Daniel had a dream and visions of his head upon his bed: then he wrote the dream, and told the sum of the matters. ²Daniel spake and said, I saw in my vision by night, and, behold, the four winds of the heaven strove upon the great sea. ³And four great beasts came up form the sea, diverse one from another. ⁴The first was like a lion, and had eagle's wings: I beheld till the wings thereof were plucked, and it was lifted up from the earth, and made stand upon the feet was a man, and a man's heart was given to it. ⁵And behold another beast, a second, like to a bear, and it raised up itself on one side, and it had three ribs in the mouth of it between the teeth of it: and they said thus unto it, Arise, devour much flesh. ⁶After this I beheld, and lo another, like a leopard, which had upon the back of it four wings of a fowl; the beast had also four heads; and dominion was given to it. ⁷After this I saw in the night visions, and behold a fourth beast, dreadful and terrible, and strong exceedingly; and it had great iron teeth: it devoured and brake in pieces, and stamped the residue with the feet of it: and it was diverse from all the beasts that were before it; and it had ten horns. ⁸I considered the horns, and, behold, there came up among them another little horn, before whom there were three of the first horns plucked up by the roots: and, behold, in this horn were eyes like the eyes of man, and a mouth speaking great things.

nd it tell out, as they watched a fit time, she went in as before with two maids only, and she was desirous to wash herself in the garden: for it was hot. [16]And there was no body there save the two elders, that had hid themselves, and watched her. [17]Then she said to her maids, Bring me oil and washing balls, and shut the garden doors, that I may wash me. [18]And they did as she bede them, and shut the garden doors, and went out themselves at privy doors to fetch the things that she had commanded them: but they saw not the elders, because they were hid. [19]Now when the maids were gone forth, the two elders rose up, and ran unto her, saying, [20]Behold, the garden doors are shut, that no man can see us, and we are in love with thee; therefore consent unto us, and lie with us. [21]If thou wilt not, we will bear witness against thee, that a young man was with thee: and therefore thou didst send away thy maids from thee. [22]Then Susanna sighed, and said, I am straitened on every side: for if I do this thing, it is death unto me: and if I do it not, I cannot escape your hands. [23]It is better for me to fall into your hands, and not do it, than to sin in the sight of the LORD.

nd in that same place there was a great dragon, which they of Babylon worshipped. [24]And the king said unto Daniel, Wilt thou also say that this is of brass? lo he liveth, he eateth and drinketh; thou cast not say that he is no living god: therefore worship him. [25]Then said Daniel unto the king, I will worship the Lord my God: for he is the living God. [26]But give me leave, O king, and I shall slay this dragon without sword or staff. The king said, I give thee leave. [27]Then Daniel took pitch, and fat, and hair, and did seethe them together, and made lumps thereof: this he put in the dragon's mouth, and so the dragon burst in sunder: and Daniel said, lo, these are the gods ye worship.

he word of the LORD that came unto Hosea, the son of Beeri, in the days of Uzziah, Jotham, Ahaz, and Hezekiah, kings of Judah, and in the days of Jeroboam the son of Joash, king of Israel. [2]The beginning of the word of the LORD by Hosea. And the LORD said to Hosea, Go, take unto thee a wife of whoredoms and children of whoredoms: for the land hath committed great whoredom, departing from the LORD. [3]So he went and took Gomer the daughter of Diblaim; which conceived, and bare him a son. [4]And the LORD said unto him, Call his name Jezreel; for yet a little while, and I will avenge the blood of Jezreel upon the house of Jehu, and will cause to cease the kingdom of the house of Israel. [5]And it shall come to pass at that day, that I will break the bow of Israel in the valley of Jezreel. [6]And she conceived again, and bare a daughter. And God said unto him, Call her name Lorhamah: for I will no more have mercy upon the house of Israel; but I will utterly take them away. [7]But I will have mercy upon the house of Judah, and will save them by the LORD their God, and will not save them by bow, nor by sword, nor by battle, by horses, nor by horsemen. [8]Now when she had weaned Loruhamah, she conceived, and bare a son. [9]Then said God, Call his name Loammi: for ye are not my people, and I will not be your God.

nd it shall come to pass afterward, that I will pour out my spirit upon all flesh; and your sons and your daughters shall prophesy, your old men shall dream dreams, your young men shall see visions: ²⁹And also upon the servants and upon the handmaids in those days will I pour out my spirit. ³⁰And I will shew wonders in the heavens and in the earth, blood, and fire, and pillars of smoke. ³¹The sun shall be turned into darkness, and the moon into blood, before the great and the terrible day of the Lord come. ³²And it shall come to pass, that whosoever shall call on the name of the Lord shall be delivered: for in mount Zion and in Jerusalem shall be deliverance, as the Lord hath said, and in the remnant whom the Lord shall call.

hen Jonah prayed unto the LORD his God out of the fish's belly, [2]And said, I cried by reason of mine affliction unto the LORD, and he heard me; out of the belly of hell cried I, and thou heardest my voice. [3]For thou hadst cast me into the deep, in the midst of the seas; and the floods compassed me about: all thy billows and thy waves passed over me. [4]Then I said, I am cast out of thy sight; yet I will look again toward thy holy temple. [5]The waters compassed me about, even to the soul: the dipth closed me round about, the weeds were wrapped about my head. [6]I went down to the bottoms of the mountains; the earth with her bars was about me for even: yet hast thou brought up my life from corruption. O LORD my God. [7]When my soul fainted within me I remembered the LORD: and my prayer came in unto thee, into thine holy temple. [8]They that observe lying vanities forsake their own mercy. [9]But I will sacrifice unto thee with the voice of thanksgiving; I will pay that that I have vowed. Salvation is of the LORD. [10]And the LORD spake unto the fish, and it vomited out Jonah upon the dry land.

So Jonah went out of the city, and sat on the east side of the city, and there made him a booth, and sat under it in the shadow, till he might see what would become of the city. ⁶And the LORD God prepared a gourd, and made it to come up over Jonah, that it might be a shadow over his head, to deliver him from his grief. So Jonah was exceeding glad of the gourd. ⁷But God prepared a worm when the morning rose the next day, and it smote the gourd that it withered. ⁸And it came to pass, when the sun did arise, that God prepared a vehement east wind; and the sun beat upon the head of Jonah, that he fainted, and wished in himself to die, and said, It is better for me to die than to live. ⁹And God said to Jonah, Doest thou well to be angry for the gourd? And he said, I do well to be angry, even unto death. ¹⁰Then said the LORD, Thou hast had pity on the gourd, for the which thou hast not labored, neither madest it grow; which came up in a night, and perished in a night: ¹¹And should not I spare Niniveh, that great city, wherein are more than sixscore thousand persons that cannot discern between their right hand and their left hand; and also much cattle?

ut thou, Bethlehem Ephrtah, though thou be little among the thousands of Judah, yet out of thee shall he come forth unto me that is to be ruler in Israel; whose goings forth have been from of old, from everlasting. ³Therefore will he give them up, until the time that she which travaileth hath brought forth: then the remnant of his brethren shall return unto the children of Israel. ⁴And he shall stand and feed in the strenth of the LORD, in the majesty of the name of the LORD his God; and they shall abide: for now shall he be great unto the ends of the earth. ⁵And this man shall be the peace, when the Assyrian shall come into our land: and when he shall tread in our palaces, then shall we raise against him seven shepherds, and eight principal men. ⁶And they shall waste the land of Assyria with the sword, and the land of Nimrod in the entrances thereof: thus shall he deliver us from the Assyrian, when he cometh into our land, and when he readeth within our borders.

rt thou not from everlasting, O Lord my God, mine Holy One? we shall not die. O Lord, thou hast ordained them for judgment; and, O mighty God, thou hast established them for correction. ¹³Thou art of purer eyes than to behold evil, and canst not look on iniquity: wherefore lookest thou upon them that deal treacherously, and holdest thy tongue when the wicked devoureth the man that is more righteous than he? ¹⁴And makest men as the fishes of the sea, as the creeping things, that have no ruler over them? ¹⁵They take up all of them with the angle, they catch them in their net, and gather them in their drag: therefore they rejoice and are glad. ¹⁶Therefore they sacrifice unto their net, and burn incense unto their drag; because by them their portion is fat, and their meat plenteous. ¹⁷Shall they therefore empty their net, and not spare continually to slay the nations?

ejoice greatly, O daughter of Zion; shout, O daughter of Jerusalem: behold, thy King cometh unto thee: he is just, and having salvation: lowly, and riding upon an ass, and upon a colt the foal of an ass. [10]And I will cut off the chariot form Ephraim, and the horse from Jerusalem, and the battle bow shall be cut off: and he shall speak peace unto the heathen: and his dominion shall be from sea even to sea, and from the river even to the ends of the earth.

hen she came to the pillar of the bed, which was at Holofernes' head, and took down his fauchion from thence, [7]and approached to his bed, and took hold of the hair of his head, and said, Strengthen me, O Lord God of Israel, this day. [8]And she smote twice upon his neck with all her might, and she took away his head from him, [9]And tumbled his body down from the bed, and pulled down the canopy from the pillars; and anon after she went forth, and gave Holofernes his head to her maid; [10]And she put it in her bag of meat: so they twain went together according to their custom unto prayer: and when they passed the camp, they compassed the valley, and went up the mountain of Bethulia, and came to the gates thereof. [11]Then said Judith afar off to the watchmen at the gate, Open, open now the gate: God, even our god, is with us, to shew his power yet in Jerusalem, and his forces against the enemy, as he hath even done this day.

ut he came again, and said, Father, one of our nation is strangled, and is cast out in the marketplace. ⁴Then before I had tasted of any meat, I started up, and took him up into a room until the going down of the son. ⁵Then I returned, and washed myself, and ate my meat in heaviness, ⁶Remembering, that prophecy of Amos, as he said, Your feasts shall be turned into mourning, and all your mirth into lamentation. ⁷Therefore I wept: and after the going down of the sun I went and made a grave and buried him. ⁸But my neighbors mocked me, and said, This man is not yet afraid to be put to death for this matter: who fled away; and yet, lo, he burieth the dead again. ⁹The same night also I returned from the burial, and slept by the wall of my courtyard, being polluted, and my face was uncovered: ¹⁰And I knew not that there were sparrows in the wall, and mine eyes being open, the sparrows muted warm dung into mine eyes; and a whiteness came in mine eyes; and I went to the physicians, but they helped me not: moreover Achiacharus did nourish me, until I went into Elymais.

nd as they went on their journey, they came in the evening to the river Tigris, and they lodged there. [2]And when the young man went down to wash himself, a fish leaped out of the river, and would have devoured him. [3]Then the angel said unto him, Take the fish. And the young man laid hold of the fish, and drew it to land. [4]To whom the angel said, Open the fish, and take the heart and the liver and the gall, and put them up safely. [5]So the young man did as the angel commanded him; and when they had roasted the fish, they did eat it: then they both went of their way, till they drew near to Ecbatane. [6]Then the young man said to the angel, Brother Azarias, to what use is the heart and the liver and the gall of the fish? [7]And he said unto him, Touching the heart and the liver, if a devil or an evil spirit trouble any, we must make a smoke thereof before the man of the woman, and the party shall be more vexed. [8]As for the gall, it is good to anoint a man that hath whiteness in his eyes, and he shall be healed.

nd when she espied him coming, she said to his father, Behold, thy son cometh, and the man that went with him. [7]Then said Raphael, I know, Tobias, that thy father will open his eyes. [8]Therefore anoint thou his eyes with the gall, and being pricked therewith, he shall rub, and the whiteness shall fall away, and he shall see thee. [9]Then Anna ran forth, and fell upon the neck of her son, and said unto him, Seeing I have seen thee, my son, from heceforth I am conent to die. And they wept both. [10]Tobit also went forth toward the door, and stumbled: but his son ran unto him, [12]And when his eyes began to smart, he rubbed them; [13]And the whiteness pilled away from the corners of his eyes: and when he saw his son, he fell upon his neck. [14]And he wept, and said, Blessed art thou, O God, and blessed is thy name for ever; and blessed are all thine holy angels: [15]For thou hast scourged, and hast taken pity on me: for, behold, I see my son Tobias. And his son went in rejoicing, and told his father the great things that had happened to him in Media.

ow when he had left speaking these words, there came one of the Jews in the sight of all to sacrifice on the altar which was at Modin, according to the king's commandment. [24]Which thing when Mattathias saw, he was inflamed with zeal, and his reins tembled, neither could he forbear to shew his anger according to judgment: wherefore he ran, and slew him upon the altar. [25]Also the king's commissioner, who compelled men to sacrifice, he killed at that time, and the altar he pulled down. [26]Thus dealt he zealously for the law of God, like as Phinees did unto Zambri the son of Salom. [27]And Mattathias cried throughout the city with a loud voice, saying, Whosoever is zealous of the law, and maintaineth the covenant, let him follow me. [28]So he and his sons fled into the mountains, and left all that ever they had in the city.

his done, Judas returned again with his host from pursuing them, [17]And said to the people, Be not greedly of the spoils, inasmuch as there is a battle before us, [18]And Gorgias and his host are here by us in the mountain: But stand ye now against our enemies, and overcome them, and after this ye may boldly take the spoils. [19]As Judas was yet speaking these words, there appeared a part of them looking out of the mountain: [20]Who when they perceived that the Jews had put their host to flight, and were burning the tents; for the smoke that was seen declared what was done: [21]When therefore they perceived these things, they were sore afraid, and seeing also the host of Judas in the plain ready to fight, [22]They fled every one into the land of strangers. [23]Then Judas returned to spoil the tents, where they got much gold, and silver, and blue silk, and purple of the sea, and great riches.

[24]After this they went home, and sung a song of thanksgiving, and praised the LORD in heaven: because it is good, because his mercy endureth for ever. [25]Thus Israel had a great deliverance that day.

hen the king's army went up to Jerusalem to meet them, and the king pitched his tents against Judea, and against mount Sion. ⁴⁹But with them that were in Bethsura he made peace: for they came out of the city, because they had no victuals there to endure the siege, it being a year of rest to the land. ⁵⁰So the king took Bethsura, and set a garrison there to keep it. ⁵¹As for the sanctuary, he besieged it many days: and set there artillery with engines and instruments to cast fire and stones, and pieces to cast darts and slings. ⁵²Whereupon they also made engines, and held them battle a long season. ⁵³Yet at the last, their vessels being without victuals, (for that it was the seventh year, and they in Judea, that were delivered from the Gentiles, had eaten up the residue of the store;) ⁵⁴There were but a few left in the sanctuary, because the famine did so prevail against them, that they were fain to disperse themselves, every man to his own place.

So when Jonathan heard these words of Apollonius, he was moved in his mind, and choosing ten thousand men he went out of Jerusalem, where Simon his brother met him for to help him. ⁷⁵And he pitched his tents against Joppe: but they of Joppe shut him out of the city, because Apollonius had a garrison there. ⁷⁶Then Jonathan laid siege unto it: whereupon they of the city let him in for fear: and so Jonathan won Joppe. ⁷⁷Whereof when Apollonius heard, he took three thousand horsemen, with a great host of footmen, and went to Azotus as one that journeyed, and therewithal drew him forth into the plain, because he had a great number of horsemen, in whom he put his trust. ⁷⁸Then Jonathan followed after him to Azotus, where the armies joined battle. ⁷⁹Now Apollonius had left a thousand horsemen in ambush. ⁸⁰And Jonathan knew that there was an ambushment behind him; for they had compassed in his host, and cast darts at the people, from morning till evening. ⁸¹But the people stood still, as Jonathan had commanded them: and so the enemies' horses were tired. ⁸²Then brought Simon forth his host, and set them against the footmen, (for the horsemen were spent,) who were discomfited by him, and fled.

evertheless Heliodorus executed that which was decreed. ²⁴Now as he was there present himself with his guard about the treasury, the LORD of spirits, and the Prince of all power, caused a great apparition, so that all that presumed to come in with him were astonished at the power of God, and fainted, and were sore afraid. ²⁵For there appeared unto them an horse with a terrible rider upon him and adorned with a very fair covering, and he ran fiercely, and smote at Heliodorus with his forefeet, and it seemed that he that sat upon the horse had complete harness of gold. ²⁶Moreover two other young men appeard before him, notable in strength, excellent in beauty, and comely in apparel, who stood by him on either side, and scourged him continually, and gave him many sore stripes. ²⁷And Heliodorus fell suddenly unto the ground, and was compassed with great darkness: but they that were with him took him up, and put him into a litter. ²⁸Thus him, that lately came with a great train and with all his guard into the said treasury, they carried out, being unable to help himself with his weapons: and manifestly they acknowledged the power of God: ²⁹For he by the hand of God was cast down, and lay speechless without all hope of life.

bout the same time Antiochus prepared his second voyage into Egypt: [2]And then it happened, that thourgh all the city, for the space almost of forty days, there were seen horsemen running in the air, in cloth of gold, and armed with lances, like a band of soldiers, [3]And troops of hosemen in array encountering and running one against another, with shaking of shields, and multitude of pikes, and drawing of swords, and casting of darts, and glittering of golden ornaments, and harness of all sorts. [4]Wherefore every man prayed that that apparition might turn to good.

t came to pass also, that seven brethren with their mother were taken, and compelled by the king against the law to taste swine's flesh, and were tormented with scourges and whips. [2]But one of them that spake first said thus, What wouldest thou ask or learn of us? we are ready to die, rather than to transgress the laws of our fathers. [3]Then the king, being in a rage, commanded pans and caldrons to be made hot: [4]Which forthwith being hearted, he commanded to cut out the tongue of him that spake first, and to cut off the utmost parts of his body, the rest of his brethren and his mother looking on. [5]Now when he was thus maimed in all his members, he commanded him being yet alive to be brought to the fire, and to be fried in the pan: and as the vavor of the pan was for a good space dispersed, they echorted one another with the mother to die manfully.

ut the LORD Almighty, the God of Israel, smote him with an incurable and invisible plague: for as soon as he had spoken these words, a pain of the bowels that was remediless came upon him, and sore torments of the inner parts; ⁶And that most justly: for he had tormented other men's bowels with many and strange torments. ⁷Howbeit he nothing at all ceased from his bragging, but still was filled with pride, breathing out fire in his rage against the Jews, and commanding to haste the jouney: but it came to pass that he fell down from his chariot, carried violently; so that having a sore fall, all the members of his body were much pained. ⁸And thus he that a little afore thought he might command the waves of the sea, (so proud was he beyond the condition of man) and weigh the high mountains in a balance, was now cast on the ground, and carried in an horselitter, shewing forth unto all the manifest power of God. ⁹So that the worms rose up out of the body of this wicked man, and whiles he lived in sorrow and pain, his flesh fell away, and the filthiness of his smell was noisome to all his army. ¹⁰And the man, that thought a little afore he could reach to the stars of heaven, no man could endure to carry for his intolerable stink.

e went also about to make a bridge to a certain strong city, which was fenced about with walls, and inhabited by people of divers countries; and the name of it was Caspis. ¹⁴But they that were within it put such trust in the strength of the walls and provision of victuals, that they behaved themselves rudely toward them that were with Judas, railing and blaspheming, and uttering such words as were not to be spoken. ¹⁵Wherefore Judas with his company, calling upon the great LORD of the world, who without any rams of engines of war did cast down Jericho in the time of Joshua, gave a fierce assault against the walls, ¹⁶And took the city by the will of God, and made unspeakable slaughters, insomuch that a lake two furlongs broad near adjoining thereunto, being filled full, was seen running with blood.

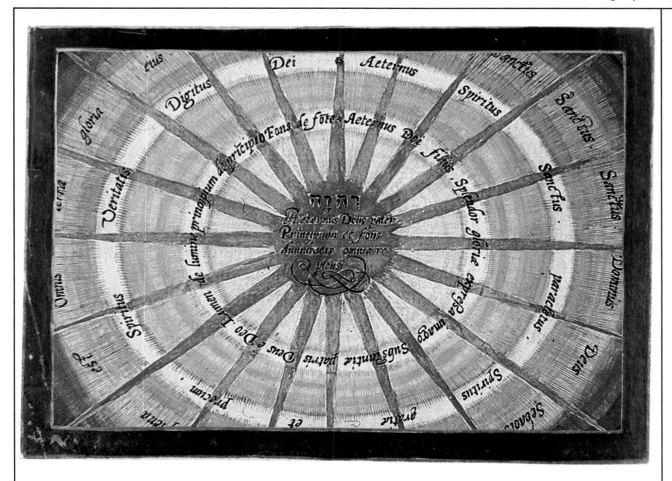

od is our refuge and strength, a very present help in trouble. [2]Therefore will not we fear, though the earth be removed, and though the mountains be carried into the midst of the sea; [3]Though the waters thereof roar and be troubled, though the mountains shake with the swelling thereof. Selah. [4]There is a river, the streams whereof shall make glad the city of God, the holy place of the tabernacles of the most High. [5]God is in the midst of her; she shall not be moved: god shall help her, and that right early. [6]The heathen raged, the kingdoms were moved: he uttered his voice, the earth melted. [7]The LORD of hosts is with us; the God of Jacob is our refuge. Selah. [8]Come, behold the works of the LORD, what desolations he hath made in the earth. [9]He maketh wars to cease unto the end of the earth; he breaketh the bow, and cutteth the spear in sunder; he burneth the chariot in the fire. [10]Be still, and know that I am God: I will be exalted among the heathen, I will be exalted in the earth. [11]The LORD of hosts is with us; the God of Jacob is our refuge. Selah.

The Art of
the New Testament

Matthäus Merian fecit 1627.

ccording to old ecclesiastical belief, Matthew is assumed to have composed the first gospel. He is said to have written it in Palestine for those Christians who had converted from Judaism. According to Papias, the early Christian writer, Matthew made a collection of Jesus' sayings in Hebrew/Aramaic. The final form of the first gospel though, is in Greek. Therefore many scholars today maintain that it was not the first gospel nor was it written in its final Greek form, by the apostle Matthew. In the New Testament, Matthew is said to have been a tax-collector (publican) in Kafanaum, from where he was called upon by Jesus to become his disciple. His attributes, a money bag and a round abacus were remainders of his former occupation as tax collector. Other traditions about his later life are, that he worked in the "Land of the Moors" (Ethiopia, Parthia, Persia), where he was killed before the altar by one of the King's slaves. The evangelistic symbol for Matthew is the "Angel".

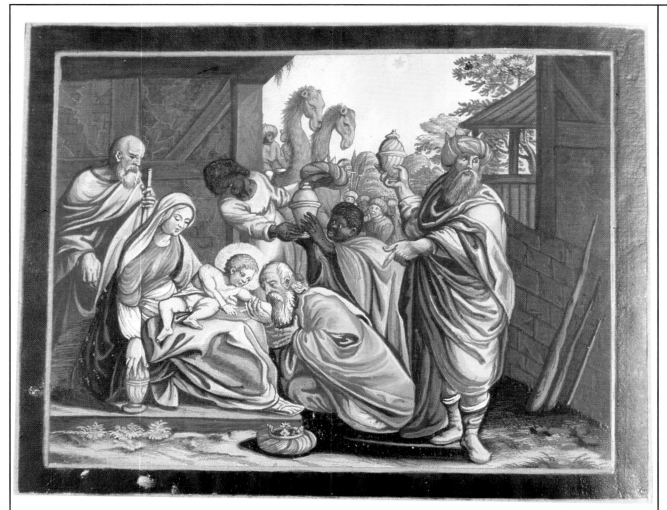

ow when Jesus was born in Bethlehem of Judea in the days of Herod the king, behold, there came wise men from the east to Jerusalem, ²Saying, Where is he that is born King of the Jews? for we have seen his star in the east, and are come to worship him. ³When Herod the king had heard these things, he was troubled, and all Jerusalem with him. ⁴And when he had gathered all the chief priests and scribes of the people together, he demanded of them where Christ should be born. ⁵And they said unto him, In Bethlehem of Judea: for thus it is written by the prophet, ⁶And thou Bethlehem, in the land of Juda, art not the least among the princes of Juda: for out of thee shall come a Governor, that shall rule my people Israel. ⁷Then Herod, when he had privily called the wise men, inquired of them diligently what time the star appeared. ⁸And he sent them to Bethlehem, and said, Go and search diligently for the young child; and when ye have found him, bring me word again, that I may come and worship him also. ⁹When they had heard the king they departed; and, Lo, the star which they saw in the east, went before them, till it came and stood over where the young child was. ¹⁰When they saw the star, they rejoiced with exceeding great joy. ¹¹And when they were come into the house, they saw the young child with Mary his mother, and fell down, and worshipped him: and when they had opened their treasures, they presented unto him gifts; gold, and frankincense, and myrrh. ¹²And being warned of God in a dream that they should not return to Herod, they departed into their own country another way.

hen cometh Jesus from Galilee to Jordan unto John, to be baptized of him. [14]But John forbade him, saying I have need to be baptized of thee and comest thou to me? [15]And Jesus answering said unto him, Suffer it to be so now for thus it becometh us to fulfil all righteousness. Then he suffered him. [16]And Jesus, when he was baptized, went up straight way out of the water: and, lo, the heavens were opened unto him, and he saw the Spirit of God descending like a dove, and lighting upon him: [17]And lo a voice from heaven, saying, This is my beloved Son, in whom I am well pleased.

he same day went Jesus out of the house, and sat by the sea side. [2]And great multitudes were gathered together unto him, so that he went into a ship, and sat; and the whole multitude stood on the shore. [3]And he spake many things unto them in parables, saying, Behold, a sower went forth to sow; [4]And when he sowed, some seeds fell by the way side, and the fowls came and devoured them up: [5]Some fell upon stony places, where they had not much earth: and forthwith they sprung up, because they had no deepness of earth: [6]And when the sun was up, they were scorched; and because they had no root, they withered away. [7]And some fell among thorns; and the thorns sprung up, and choked them: [8]But other fell into good ground, and brought forth fruit, some an hundredfold, some sixtyfold, some thirtyfold. [9]Who hath ears to hear, let him hear.

nd straightway Jesus constrained his disciples to get into a ship, and to go before him unto the other side, while he sent the multitudes away. ²³And when he had sent the multitudes away, he went up into a mountain apart to pray: and when the evening was come, he was there alone. ²⁴But the ship was now in the midst of the sea, tossed with waves: for the wind was contrary. ²⁵And in the fourth watch of the night Jesus went unto them, walking on the sea. ²⁶And when the disciples saw him walking on the sea, they were troubled, saying, It is a spirit; and they cried out for fear. ²⁷But straightway Jesus spake unto them, saying, Be of good cheer; it is I; be not afraid. ²⁸And Peter answered him and said, Lord, if it be thou, bid me come unto thee on the water. ²⁹And he said, Come. And when Peter was come down out of the ship, he walked on the water, to go to Jesus. ³⁰But when he saw the wind boisterous, he was afraid; and beginning to sink, he cried, saying, Lord, save me. ³¹And immediately Jesus stretched forth his hand, and caught him, and said unto him, O thou of little faith, wherefore didst thou doubt? ³²And when they were come into the ship, the wind ceased. ³³Then they that were in the ship came and worshipped him, saying, Of a truth thou art the Son of God.

hen Jesus went thence, and departed into the coasts of Tyre and Sidon. ²²And, behold, a woman of Canaan came out of the same coasts, and cried unto him, saying, Have mercy on me, O Lord, thou son of David; my daughter is grievously vexed with a devil. ²³But he answered her not a word. And his disciples came and besought him, saying, Send her away; for she crieth after us. ²⁴But he answered and said; I am not sent but unto the lost sheep of the house of Israel. ²⁵Then came she and worshipped him, saying, Lord, help me. ²⁶But he answered and said, It is not meet to take the children's bread, and to cast it to dogs. ²⁷And she said, Truth, Lord: yet the dogs eat of the crumbs which fall from their master's table. ²⁸Then Jesus answered and said unto her, O woman, great is thy faith: be it unto thee even as thou wilt. And her daughter was made whole from that very hour.

And after six days Jesus taketh Peter, James, and John his brother, and bringeth them up into an high mountain apart, [2]And was transfigured before them: and his face did shine as the sun, and his raiment was white as the light. [3]And, behold, there appeared unto them Moses and Elias talking with him. [4]Then answered Peter, and said unto Jesus, LORD, it is good for us to be here: if thou wilt, let us make here three tabernacles; one for thee, and one for Moses, and one for Elias. [5]While he yet spake, behold, a bright cloud overshadowed them: and behold a voice out of the cloud, which said, This is my beloved Son, in whom I am well pleased; hear ye him. [6]And when the disciples heard it, they fell on their face and were sore afraid. [7]And Jesus came and touched them, and said, Arise, and be not afraid. [8]And when they had lifted up their eyes, they saw no man, save Jesus only. [9]And as they came down from the mountain, Jesus charged them, saying, Tell the vision to no man, until the Son of man be risen again from the dead.

For the kingdom of heaven is like unto a man that is an householder, which went out early in the morning to hire laborers into his vineyard. ²And when he had agreed with the laborers for a penny a day, he sent them into his vineyard. ³And he went out about the third hour, and saw others standing idle in the marketplace, ⁴And said unto them; Go ye also into the vineyard, and whatsoever is right I will give you. And they went their way. ⁵Again he went out about the sixth and ninth hour, and did likewise. ⁶And about the eleventh hour he went out, and found others standing idle, and saith unto them, Why stand ye here all the day idle? ⁷They say unto him, Because no man hath hired us. He saith unto them, Go ye also into the vineyard; and whatsoever is right, that shall ye receive. ⁸So when even was come, the lord of the vineyard saith unto his steward, Call the laborers, and give them their hire, beginning from the last unto the first. ⁹And when they came that were hired about the eleventh hour, they received every man a penny. ¹⁰But when the first came, they supposed that they should have received more; and they likewise received every man a penny. ¹¹And when they had received it, they murmured against the goodman of the house, ¹²Saying, These last have wrought but one hour, and thou hast made them equal unto us, which have borne the burden and heat of the day. ¹³But he answered one of them, and said, Friend, I do thee no wrong: didst not thou agree with me for a penny? ¹⁴Take that thine is, and go thy way: I will give unto this last, even as unto thee. ¹⁵Is it not lawful for me to do what I will with mine own? Is thine eye evil, because I am good? ¹⁶So the last shall be first, and the first last: for many be called, but few chosen.

nd Jesus answered and spake unto them again by parables, and said, [2]The kindgom of heaven is like unto a certain king, which made a marriage for his son, [3]And sent forth his servants to call them that were bidden to the wedding: and they would not come. [4]Again, he sent forth other servants, saying, Tell them which are bidden, Behold, I have prepared my dinner: my oxen and my fatlings are killed, and all things are ready: come unto the marriage. [5]But they made light of it, and went their ways, one to his farm, another to his merchandise: [6]And the remnant tool his servants, and entreated them spitefully, and slew them. [7]But when the king heard thereof, he was wroth; and he sent forth his armies, and destroyed those murderers, and burned up their city. [8]Then saith he to his servants, The wedding is ready, but they which were bidden were not worthy. [9]Go ye therefore into the highways, and as many as ye shall find, bid to the marriage. [10]So those servants went out into the highways, and gathered together all as many as they found, both bad and good: and the wedding was furnished with guest. [11]And when the king came in to see the guests, he saw there a man which had not on a wedding garment: [12]And he saith unto him, Friend, how camest thou in hither not having a wedding garment? And he was speechless. [13]Then said the king to the servants, Bind him hand and foot, and take him away, and cast him into outer darkness; there shall be weeping and gnashing of teeth. [14]For many are called, but few are chosen.

And so he that had received five talents came and brought other five talents, saying, Lord, Thou deliveredst unto me five talents: behold, I have gained beside them five talents more. [21]His lord said unto him, Well done, thou good and faithful over a few things, I will make thee ruler over many things: enter thou into the joy of thy lord. [22]He also that had received two talents came and said, Lord, thou deliveredst unto me two talents: behold, I have gained two other talents beside them. [23]His lord said unto him, Well done, good and faithful servant; thou hast been faithful over a few things, I will make thee ruler over many things: enter thou into the joy of thy lord. [24]Then he which had received the one talent came and said, Lord, I knew thee that thou art an hard man, reaping where thou hast not sown, and gathering where thou hast not strawed: [25]And I was afraid, and went and hid thy talent in the earth: lo, there thou hast that is thine. [26]His lord answered and said unto him, Thou wicked and slothful servant, thou knewest that I reap where I sowed not, and gather where I have not strawed. [27]Thou oughtest therefore to have put my money to the exchangers, and then at my coming I should have received mine own with usury. [28]Take therefore the talent from him, and give it unto him which hath ten talents. [29]For unto every one that hath shall be given, and he shall have abundance: but from him that hath not shall be taken away even that which he hath. [30]And cast ye the unprofitable servant into outer darkness: there shall be weeping and gnashing of teeth.

hen the Son of man shall come in his glory, and all the holy angels with him, then shall he sit upon the throne of his glory: ³²And before him shall be gathered all nations: and he shall separate them one from another, as a shepherd divideth his sheep from the goats: ³³And he shall set the sheep on his right hand, but the goats on the left. ³⁴Then shall the King say unto them on his right hand, come, ye blessed of my Father, inherit the kingdom prepared for you from the foundation of the world: ³⁵For I was a hungered, and ye gave me meat: I was thirsty, and ye gave me drink: I was a stranger, and ye took me in: ³⁶Naked, and ye clothed me: I was sick, and ye visited me: I was in prison, and ye came unto me. ³⁷Then shall the righteous answer him, saying, Lord, when saw we thee a hungered, and fed thee? or thirsty, and gave thee drink? ³⁸When saw we thee a stranger, and took thee in? or naked, and clothed thee? ³⁹Or when saw we thee sick, or in prison, and came unto thee? ⁴⁰And the King shall answer and say unto them, Verily I say unto you, Inasmuch as ye have done it unto one of the least of these my brethren, ye have done it unto me.

ow when the even was come, he sat down with the twelve. [21]And as they did eat, he said, Verily I say unto you, that one of you shall betray me. [22]And they were exceeding sorrowful, and began every one of them to say unto him, Lord, is it I? [23]And he answered and said, He that dippeth his hand with me in the dish, the same shall betray me. [24]The Son of man goeth as it is written of him: but woe unto that man by whom the Son of man is betrayed! it had been good for that man if he had not been good for that man if he had not been born. [25]Then Judas, which betrayed him, answered and said, Master, is it I? He said unto him, Thou hast said. [26]And as they were eating, Jesus took bread, and blessed it, and brake it, and gave it to the disciples, and said, Take, eat; this is my body.

hen cometh Jesus with them unto a place called Gethsemane, and saith unto the disciples, Sit ye here, while I go and pray yonder. [37]And he took with him Peter and the two sons of Zebedee, and began to be sorrowful and very heavy. [38]Then saith he unto them, My soul is exceeding sorrowful, even unto death: tarry ye here, and watch with me. [39]And he went a little farther, and fell on his face, and prayed, saying, O my Father, if it be possible, let this cup pass from me: nevertheless not as I will, but as thou wilt. [40]And he cometh unto the disciples, and findeth them asleep, and saith unto Peter, What, could ye not watch with me one hour? [41]Watch and pray, that ye enter not into temptation: the spirit indeed is willing, but the flesh is weak. [42]He went away again the second time, and prayed, saying, O my Father, if this cup may not pass away from me, except I drink it, thy will be done. [43]And he came and found them asleep again: for their eyes were heavy. [44]And he left them, and went away again, and prayed the third time, saying the same words. [45]Then cometh he to his disciples, and saith unto them, Sleep on now, and take your rest: behold, the hour is at hand, and the Son of man is betrayed into the hands of sinners. [46]Rise, let us be going: behold, he is at hand that doth betray me.

And while he yet spake, lo, Judas, one of the twelve, came, and with him a great multitude with swords and staves, from the chief priests and elders of the people. ⁴⁸Now he that betrayed him gave them a sign, saying, Whomsoever I shall kiss, that same is he: hold him fast. ⁴⁹And forthwith he came to Jesus, and said, Hail, master; and kissed him. ⁵⁰And Jesus said unto him, Friend, wherefore art thou come? Then came they, and laid hands on Jesus, and took him. ⁵¹And, behold, one of them which were with Jesus stretched out his hand, and drew his sword, and struck a servant of the high priest's, and smote off his ear. ⁵²Then said Jesus unto him, Put up again thy sword into his place: for all they that take the sword shall perish with the sword. ⁵³Thinkest thou that I cannot now pray to my Father, and he shall presently give me more that twelve legions of angels? ⁵⁴But how then shall the scriptures be fulfilled, that thus it must be? ⁵⁵In that same hour said Jesus to the multitudes, Are ye come out as against a thief with swords and staves for to take me? I sat daily with you teaching in the temple, and ye laid no hold on me. ⁵⁶But all this was done, that the scriptures of the prophets might be fulfilled. Then all the disciples forsook him, and fled.

**A**nd they that had laid hold on Jesus led him away to Caiaphas the high priest, where the scribes and the elders were assembled. [58]But Peter followed him afar off unto the high priest's palace, and went in, and sat with the servants, to see the end. [59]Now the chief priests, and elders, and all the council, sought false witness against Jesus, to put him to death; [60]But found none: yea, though many false witnesses came, yet found they none. At the last came two false witnesses, [61]And said, This fellow said, I am able to destroy the temple of God, and to build it in three days. [62]And the high priest arose, and said unto him, Answerest thou nothing? what is it which these witness against thee? [63]But Jesus held his peace. And the high priest answered and said unto him, I adjure thee by the living God, that thou tell us whether thou be the Christ, the Son of God. [64]Jesus saith unto him, Thou hast said: nevertheless I say unto you, Hereafter shall ye see the Son of man sitting on the right hand of power, and coming in the clouds of heaven. [65]Then the high priest rent his clothes, saying, He hath spoken blasphemy; what further need have we of witnesses? behold, now ye have heard his blasphemy. [66]What think ye? They answered and said, He is guilty of death. [67]Then did they spit in his face, and buffeted him; and others smote him with the palms of their hands, [68]Saying, Prophesy unto us, thou Christ, Who is he that smote thee?

ow at that feast the governor was wont to release unto the people a prisoner, whom they would. [16]And they had then a notable prisoner, called Barabbas. [17]Therefore when they were gathered together, Pilate said unto them, Whom will ye that I release unto you? Barabbas, or Jesus which is called Christ? [18]For he knew that for envy they had delivered him. [19]When he was set down on the judgment seat, his wife sent unto him, saying, Have thou nothing to do with that just man: for I have suffered many things this day in a dream because of him. [20]But the chief priests and elders persuaded the multitude that they should ask Barabbas, and destroy Jesus. [21]The governor answered and said unto them, Whether of the twain will ye that I release unto you? They said, Barabbas. [22]Pilate saith unto them, What shall I do then with Jesus which is called Christ? They all say unto him, Let him be crucified. [23]And the governor said, Why, what evil hath he done? But they cried out the more, saying, Let him be crucified. [24]When Pilate saw that he could prevail nothing, but that rather a tumult was made, he took water, and washed his hands before the multitude, saying, I am innocent of the blood of this just person: see ye to it. [25]Then answered all the people, and said, His blood be on us, and on our children. [26]Then released he Barabbas unto them: and when he had scourged Jesus, he delivered him to be crucified.

hen the soldiers of the governor took Jesus into the common hall, and gathered unto him the whole band of soldiers. [28]And they stripped him, and put on him a scarlet robe. [29]And when they had platted a crown of thorns, they put it upon his head, and a reed in his right hand: and they bowed the knee before him, and mocked him, saying, Hail, King of the Jews! [30]And they spit upon him, and took the reed, and smote him on the head. [31]And after that they had mocked him, they took the robe off from him, and put his own raiment on him, and led him away to crucify him.

nd after that they had
mocked him, they took
the robe off from him,
and put his own rai-
ment on him, and led
him away to crucify
him. [32]And as they
came out, they found a man of Cyrene, Simon
by name: him they compelled to bear his cross.
[33]And when they were come unto a place called Golgatha, that is to say, a place of a skull.
[34]They gave him vinegar to drink mingled with
gall: and when he had tasted thereof, he would
not drink.

**A**nd when they were come unto a place called Golgatha, that is to say, a place of a skull, [34]They gave him vinegar to drink mingled with gall: and when he had tasted thereof, he would not drink. [35]And they crucified him, and parted his garments, casting lots: that it might be fulfilled which was spoken by the prophet, They parted my garments among them, and upon my vesture did they cast lots. [36]And sitting down they watched him there; [37]And set up over his head his accusation written, THIS IS JESUS THE KING OF THE JEWS. [38]Then were there two thieves crucified with him, one on the right hand, and another on the left. [39]And they that passed by reviled him, wagging their heads, [40]And saying, Thou that destroyest the temple, and buildest it in three days, save thyself. If thou be the Son of God, come down from the cross. [41]Likewise also the chief priests mocking him, with the scribes and elders, said, [42]He saved others; himself he cannot save. If he be the King of Israel, let him now come down from the cross, and we will believe him. [43]He trusted in God; let him deliver him now, if he will have him: for he said, I am the Son of God. [44]The thieves also, which were crucified with him, cast the same in his teeth.

hen the even was come, there came a rich man of Arimathea, named Joseph, who also himself was Jesus' disciple: [58]He went to Pilate, and begged the body of Jesus. Then Pilate commanded the body to be delivered. [59]And when Joseph had taken the body, he wrapped it in a clean linen cloth, [60]And laid it in his own new tomb, which he had hewn out in the rock: and he rolled a great stone to the door of the sepulchre, and departed.

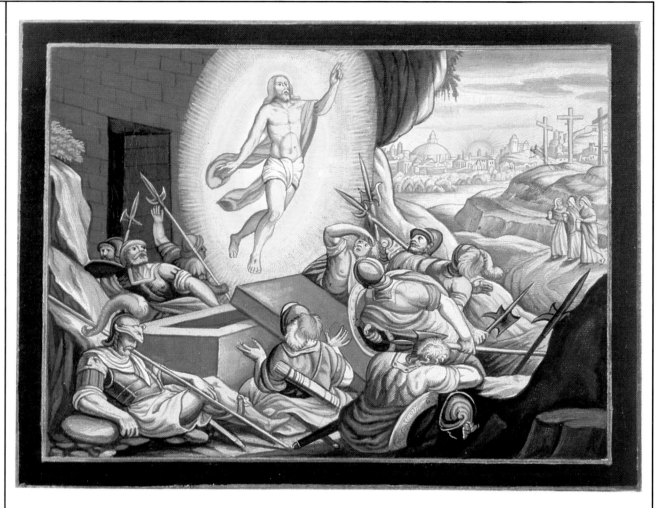

n the end of the sabbath, as it began to dawn toward the first day of the week, came Mary Magdalene and the other Mary to see the sepulchre. [2]And, behold, there was a great earthquake: for the angel of the Lord descended from heaven, and came and rolled back the stone from the door, and sat upon it. [3]His countenance was like lightning, and his raiment white snow: [4]And for fear of him the keepers did shake, and became as dead men. [5]And the angel answered and said unto the women, Fear not ye: for I know that ye seek Jesus which was crucified. [6]He is not here: for he is risen as he said. Come, see the place where the Lord lay. [7]And go quickly, and tell his disciples that he is risen from the dead; and, behold, he goeth before you into Galilee; there shall ye see him: lo, I have told you. [8]And they departed quickly from the sepulchre with fear and geat joy; and did run to bring his disciples word. [9]And as they went to tell his desciples, behold, Jesus met them saying, All hail. And they came and held him by the feet, and worshipped him. [10]Then said Jesus unto them, Be not afraid: go tell my brethren that they go into Galilee, and there shall they see me.

ark, a Jew from Jerusalem, whose full name was John Mark, is considered since the 2nd century A.D. the composer of the 2nd of the 4 gospels in the old Christian tradition. He is said to have accompanied Paul and Barnabas, his cousin, on their missionary journey to Rome, where he probably assisted both Paul and Peter. This and the fact that his name was also mentioned in the 1st Epistle of Peter, may have led Papias, bishop of Hierapolis and Church writer, to believe that John Mark was Peter's interpreter. The Gospel of St. Mark was written about 70 A.D. Mark was sent to Alexandria by orders of Peter, where he acted as bishop and died a martyr's death. Between 828-829 A.D. his relics were abducted from Alexandria to Venice by venetian merchants - one of the most famous relics' robberies of the early and late Middle Ages. Since the, Venice's claim to fame is having its own patron saint, whose symbol, the Lion of St. Mark, can still be seen everywhere in town.

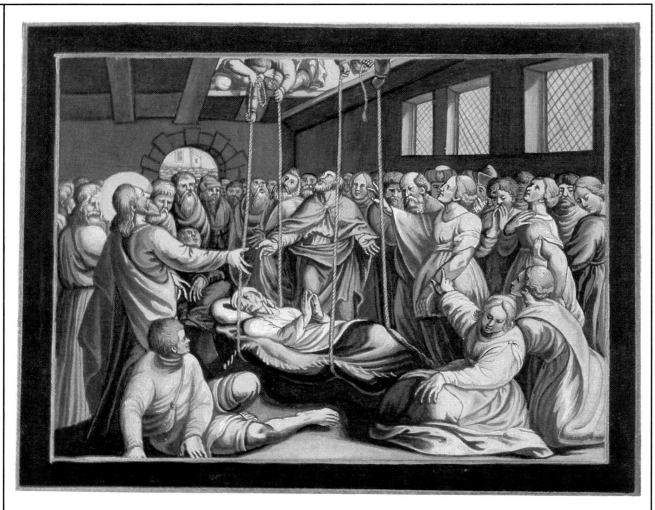

**A**nd again he entered into Capernaum after some days; and it was noised that he was in the house. [2]And straightway many were gathered together, insomuch that there was no room to receive them, no, not so much as about the door: and he preached the word unto them. [3]And they come unto him, bringing one sick of the palsy which was borne of four. [4]And when they could not come nigh unto him for the press, they uncovered the roof where he was and when they had broken it up they let down the bed wherein the sick of the palsy lay. [5]When Jesus saw their faith, he said unto the sick of the palsy, Son thy sins be forgiven thee. [6]But there were certain of the scribes sitting there, and reasoning in their hearts, [7]Why doth this man thus speak blasphemies? who can forgive sins but God only? [8]And immediately when Jesus perceived in his spirit that they so reasoned within themselves, he said unto them, Why reason ye these things in your hearts? [9]Whether is it easier to say to the sick of the palsy, Thy sins be forgiven thee; or to say, Arise, and take up thy bed and walk? [10]But that ye may know that the Son of man hath power on earth to forgive sins, (he saith to the sick of the palsy.) [11]I say unto thee, Arise, and take up thy bed, and go thy way into thine house. [12]And immediately he arose, took up the bed, and went forth before them all; insomuch that they were all amazed, and glorified god, saying, We never saw it on this fashion.

nd the same day, when the even was come, he saith unto them, Let us pass over unto the o-ther side. [36]And when they had sent away the multitude, they took him even as he was in the ship. And there were also with him other little ships. [37]And there arose a great storm of wind, and the waves beat into the ship, so that it was now full. [38]And he was in the hinder part of the ship, asleep on a pillow: and they awake him, and say unto him, Master, carest thou not that we perish? [39]And he arose, and rebuked the wind, and said unto the sea, Peace, be still. And the wind ceased, and there was a great calm. [40]And he said unto them, Why are ye so fear-ful? how is it that ye have no faith? [41]And they feared exceedingly, and said one to another, What manner of man is this, that even the wind and the sea obey him?

nd when a convenient day was come, that Herod on his birthday made a supper to his lords, high captains, and chief estates of Galiliea; [22]And when the daughter of the said Herodias came in, and danced, and pleased Herod and them that sat with him, the king said unto the damsel, Ask of me whatsoever thou wilt, and I will give it thee. [23]And he sware unto her, Whatsoever thou shalt ask of me, I will give it thee, unto the half of my kingdom. [24]And she went forth, and said unto her mother, What shall I ask? And she said, the head of John the Baptist. [25]And she came in straightway with haste unto the king, and asked, saying, I will that thou give me by and by in a charger the head of John the Baptist. [26]And the king was exceeding sorry; yet for his oath's sake, and for their sakes which sat with him, he would not reject her. [27]And immediately the king sent an executioner, and commanded his head to be brought: and he went and beheaded him in the prison, [28]And brought his head in a charger, and gave it to the damsel: and the damsel gave it to her mother. [29]And when his disciples heard of it, they came and took up his corpse, and laid it in a tomb.

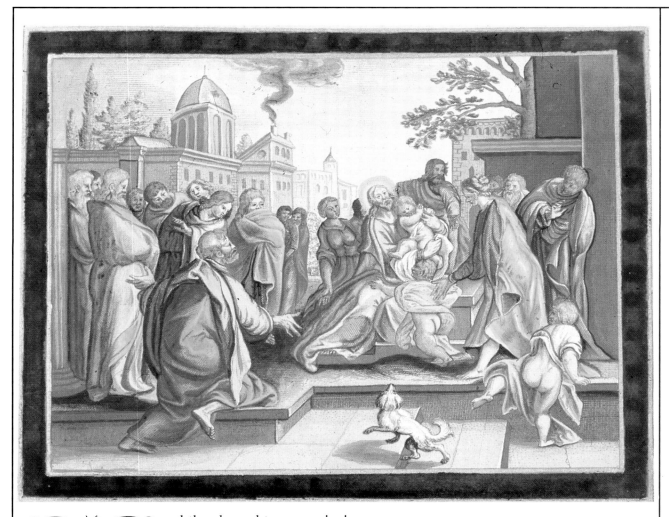

nd they brought young children to him, that he should touch them; and his disciples rebuked those that brought them. [14]But when Jesus saw it, he was much displeased, and said unto them, Suffer the little children to come unto me, and forbid them not: for of such is the kingdom of God. [15]Verily I say unto you, Whosoever shall not receive the kingdom of God as a little child, he shall not enter therein. [16]And he took them up in his arms, put his hands upon them and blessed them.

nd they brought the colt to Jesus, and cast their garments on him; and he sat upon him. [8]And many spread their garments in the way: and others cut down branches off the trees, and strawed them in the way. [9]And they that went before, and they that followed, cried, saying, Hosanna; Blessed is he that cometh in the name of the Lord: [10]Blessed be the kingdom of our father David, that cometh in the name of the Lord: Hosanna in the highest. [11]And Jesus entered into Jerusalem, and into the temple: and when he had looked round about upon all things, and now the eventide was come, he went out unto Bethany with the twelve.

nd they come to Jerusalem: and Jesus went into the temple, and began to cast out them that sold and bought in the temple, and overthrew the tables of the moneychangers, and the seats of them that sold doves; [16]And would not suffer that any man should carry any vessel through the temple. [17]And he taught, saying unto them, It is not written, My house shall be called of all nations the house of prayer? but ye have made it a den of thieves. [18]And the scribes and chief priests heard it, and sought how they might destroy him: for they feared him, because all the people were astonished at his doctrine. [19]And when even was come, he went out of the city. [20]And in the morning, as they passed by, they saw the fig tree dried up from the roots. [21]And Peter calling to remembrance saith unto him, Master, behold, the fig tree which thou cursedst is withered away.

A doctor and traveling-companion of Paul, who is mentioned three times by name as "Luke, the beloved physician" and further in II Timothy, where he is said to have helped Paul, while the latter was imprisoned. The 3rd gospel and the Acts of the Apostles are traditionally written by Luke, but contain only indirect details of his life (80 - 90 A.D.). In later arts he was portrayed with his quill and the characteristic symbol of the bull. The lengthy passages in Luke's Gospel that are dedicated to the childhood of Christ and the story of Mary, strengthen the legend according to which Luke is supposed to have painted authentical madonnas and images of Christ. Furthermore legend has it that it was Mary herself, who revealed the Gospel to Luke. The details he gives in his gospel about the Annunciation as well as precise descriptions of the birth of Jesus, could be a proof for this belief.

nd in the sixth month the angel Gabriel was sent from God unto a city of Galilee, named Nazareth, [27]To a virgin espoused to a man whose name was Joseph, of the house of David; and the virgin's name was Mary. [28]And the angel came in unto her, and said, Hail, thou that art highly favored, the Lord is with thee: blessed art thou among women. [29]And when she saw him, she was troubled at his saying, and cast in her mind what manner of salutation this should be. [30]And the angel said unto her, Fear not, Mary: for thou hast found favor with God. [31]And, behold, thou shalt conceive in thy womb, and bring forth a son, and shalt call his name JESUS. [32]He shall be great, and shall be called the Son of the Highest: and the Lord God shall give unto him the throne of his father David: [33]And he shall reign over the house of Jacob for ever; and of his kingdom there shall be no end. [34]Then said Mary unto the angel, How shall this be, seeing I know not a man? [35]And the angel answered and said unto her, The Holy Ghost shall come upon thee, and the power of the Highest shall overshadow thee: therefore also that holy thing which shall be born of thee shall be called the Son of God. [36]And, behold, thy cousin Elisabeth, she hath also conceived a son in her old age: and this is the sixth month with her, who was called barren. [37]For with God nothing shall be impossible. [38]And Mary said, Behold the handmaid of the Lord; be it unto me according to thy word. And the angel departed from her.

And there were in the same country shepherds abiding in the field, keeping watch over their flock by night. [9]And, lo, the angel of the Lord came upon them, and the glory of the Lord shone round about them: and they were sore afraid. [10]And the angel said unto them, Fear not: for, behold, I bring you good tidings of great joy, which shall be to all people. [11]For unto you is born this day in the city of David a Savior, which is Christ the Lord. [12]And this shall be a sign unto you; Ye shall find the babe wrapped in swaddling clothes, lying in a manger. [13]And suddenly there was with the angel a multitude of the heavenly host praising God, and saying, [14]Glory to God in the highest and on earth peace, good will toward men. [15]And it came to pass, as the angels were gone away from them into heaven, the shepherds said one to another, Let us now go even unto Bethlehem, and see this thing which is come to pass, which the Lord hath made known unto us. [16]And they came with haste, and found Mary, and Joseph, and the babe lying in a manger. [17]And when they had seen it, they made known abroad the saying which was told them concerning this child. [18]And all they that heard it wondered at those things which were told them by the shepherds. [19]But Mary kept all these things, and pondered them in her heart. [20]And the shepherds returned, glorifying and praising God for all the things that they had heard and seen, as it was told unto them.

nd Jesus being full of the Holy Ghost returned from Jordan, and was led by the Spirit into the wilderness, [2]Being forty days tempted of the devil. And in those days he did eat nothing: and when they were ended, he afterward hungered. [3]And the devil said unto him, If thou be the Son of God, commanded this stone that it be made bread. [4]And Jesus answered him, saying, It is written, That man shall not live by bread alone, but by every word of God.

nd he came down with them, and stood in the plain, and the company of his disciples, and a great multitude of people out of all Judea and Jerusalem, and from the sea coast of Tyre and Sidon, which came to hear him, and to be healed of their diseases; [18]And they that were vexed with unclean spirits: and they were healed. [19]And the whole multitude sought to touch him: for there went virtue out of him, and healed them all. [20]And he lifted up his eyes on his disciples, and said, Blessed be ye poor: for yours is the kingdom of God. [21]Blessed are ye that hunger now: for ye shall be filled. Blessed are ye that weep now: for ye shall laugh. [22]Blessed are ye, when men shall hate you, and when they shall separate you from their company and shall reproach you, and cast out your name as evil, for the Son of man's sake. [23]Rejoice ye in that day, and leap for joy: for, behold, your reward is great in heaven: for in the like manner did their fathers unto the prophets.

nd it came to pass the day after, that he went into a city alled Nain; and many of his disciples went with him, and much people. [12]Now when he came nigh to the gate of the city, behold, there was a dead man carried out, the only son of his mother, and she was a widow: and much people of the city was with her. [13]And when the Lord saw her, he had compassion on her, and said unto her, Weep not. [14]And he came and touched the bier: and they that bare him stood still. And he said, Young man, I say unto thee, Arise. [15]And he that was dead sat up, and began to speak. And he delivered him to his mother. [16]And there came a fear on all: and they glorified God, saying, That a great prophet is risen up among us; and, That god hath visited his people. [17]And this rumor of him went forth throughout all Judea, and througout all the region round about.

nd, behold, a woman in the city, which was a sinner, when she knew that Jesus sat at meat in the Pharisee's house, brought an alabaster box of ointment, [38]And stood at his feet behind him weeping, and began to wash his feet with tears, and did wipe them with the hairs of her head, and kissed his feet, and anointed them with the ointment. [39]Now when the Pharisee which had bidden him saw it, he spake within himself, saying, This man, if he were a prophet, would have known who and what manner of woman this is that toucheth him: for she is a sinner. [40]And Jesus answering said unto him, Simon, I have somewhat to say unto thee. And he saith, Master, say on. [41]There was a certain creditor which had two debtors: the one owed five hundred pence, and the other fifty. [42]And when they had nothing to pay, he frankly forgave them both. Tell me therefore, which of them will love him most? [43]Simon answered and said, I suppose that he, to whom he forgave most. And he said unto him, Thou hast rightly judged. [44]And he turned to the woman, and said unto Simon, Seest thou this woman? I entered into thine house, thou gavest me no water for my feet: but she hath washed my feet with tears, and wiped them with the hairs of her head. [45]Thou gavest me no kiss: but this woman since the time I came in hath not ceased to kiss my feet. [46]My head with oil thou didst not anoint: but this woman hath anointed my feet with ointment. [47]Wherefore I say unto thee, Her sins, which are many, are forgiven; for she loved much: but to whom little is forgiven, the same loveth little. [48]And he said unto her, Thy sins are forgiven.

ut he, willing to justify himself, said unto Jesus, And who is my neighbor? [30]And Jesus answering said, A certain man went down from Jerusalem to Jericho, and fell among thieves, which stripped him of his raiment, and wounded him, and departed, leaving him half dead. [31]And by chance there came down a certain priest that way: and when he saw him, he passed by on the other side. [32]And likewise a Levite, when he was at the place, came and looked on him, and passed by on the other side. [33]But a certain Samaritan, as he journeyed, came where he was: and when he saw him, he had compassion on him, [34]And went to him, and bound up his wounds, pouring in oil and wine, and set him on his own beast, and brought him to an inn, and took care of him. [35]And on the morrow when he departed, he took, out two pence, and gave them to the host, and said unto him, Take care of him; and whatsoever thou spendest more, when I come again, I will repay thee. [36]Which now of these three, thinkest thou, was neighbor unto him that fell among the thieves? [37]And he said, He that shewed mercy on him. Then said Jesus unto him, Go, and do thou likewise.

ow it came to pass, as they went, that he entered into a certain village: and a certain woman named Martha received him into her house. [39]And she had a sister called Mary, which also sat at Jesus' feet, and heard his word. [40]But Martha was cumbered about much serving, and came to him, and said, Lord, dost thou not care that my sister hath left me to serve alone? bid her therefore that she help me. [41]And Jesus answered and said unto her, Martha, Martha, thou art careful and troubled about many things: [42]But one thing is needful: and Mary hath chosen that good part, which shall not be taken away from her.

nd he was casting out a devil, and it was dumb. And it came to pass, when the devil was gone out, the dumb spake; and the people wondered. [15]But some of them said, He casteth out the devils through Beelzebub the chief of the devils. [16]And others, tempting him, sought of him a sign from heaven.

nd he arose, and came to his father. But when he was yet a great way off, his father saw him, and had compassion, and ran, and fell on his neck, and kissed him. [21]And the son said unto him, Father, I have sinned against heaven, and in thy sight, and am no more worthy to be called thy son. [22]But the father said to his servants, Bring forth the best robe, and put it on him; and put a ring on his hand, and shoes on his feet: [23]And bring hither the fatted calf, and kill it; and let us eat, and be merry: [24]For this my son was dead, and is alive again; he was lost, and is found. And they began to be merry.

 here was a certain rich man, which was clothed in purple and fine linen, and fared sumptuously every day: [20]And there was a certain beggar named Lazarus, which was laid at his gate, full of sores, [21]And desiring to be fed with the crumbs which fell from the rich man's table: moreover the dogs came and licked his sores. [22]And it came to pass, that the beggar died, and was carried by the angels into Abraham's bosom: the rich man also died, and was buried; [23]And in hell he lift up his eyes, being in torments, and seeth Abraham afar off, and Lazarus in his bosom. [24]And he cried and said, Father Abraham, have mercy on me, and send Lazarus, that he may dip the tip of his finger in water, and cool my tongue; for I am tormented in this flame. [25]But Abraham said, Son, remember that thou in thy lifetime receivedst thy good things, and likewise Lazarus evil things: but now he is comforted, and thou art tormented. [26]And beside all this, between us and you there is a great gulf fixed: so that they which would pass from hence to you cannot: neither can they pass to us, that would come from thence.

And it came to pass, as he went to Jerusalem, that he passed Galilee. ¹²And he entered into a certain village, there met him ten men that were lepers, which stood afar off: ¹³And they lifted up their voices, and said, Jesus, Master, have mercy on us. ¹⁴And when he saw them, he said unto them, Go shew yourselves unto the priests. And it came to pass, that, as they went they were cleansed. ¹⁵And one of them, when he saw that he was healed, turned back, and with a loud voice glorified God, ¹⁶And fell down on his face at his feet, giving him thanks: and he was a Samaritan. ¹⁷And Jesus answering said, Were there not ten cleansed? but where are the nine? ¹⁸There are not found that returned to give glory to God, save this stranger. ¹⁹And he said unto him, Arise, go thy way: thy faith hath made thee whole.

nd he spake this parable unto certain which trusted in themselves that they were righteous, and despised others: [10]Two men went up into the temple to pray; the one a Pharaisee, and the other a publican. [11]The Pharisee stood and prayed thus with himself, God, I thank thee, that I am not as other men are, extortioners, unjust, adulterers, or even as this publican. [12]I fast twice in the week, I give tithes of all that I possess. [13]And the publican, standing afar off, would not lift up so much as his eyes unto heaven, but smote upon his breast, saying, God be merciful to me a sinner. [14]I tell you, this man went down to his house justified rather than the other: for every one that exalteth himself shall be abased; and he that humbleth himself shall be exalted.

nd it came to pass, that as he was nigh unto Jericho, a certain blind man sat by the way side begging: [36]And hearing the multitude pass by, he asked what it meant. [37]And they told him, that Jesus of Nazareth passeth by. [38]And he cried, saying, Jesus, thou son of David, have mercy on me. [39]And they which went before rebuked him, that he should hold his peace: but he cried so much the more, Thou son of David, have mercy on me. [40]And Jesus stood, and commanded him to be brought unto him: and when he was come near, he asked him, [41]Saying, What wilt thou that I shall do unto thee? And he said, Lord, that I may receive my sight. [42]And Jesus said unto him, Receive thy sight: thy faith hath saved thee. [43]And immediately he received his sight, and followed him, glorifying God: and all the people, when they saw it, gave praise unto God.

nd Jesus entered and passed through Jericho. [2]And, behold, there was a rich man named Zaccheus, which was the chief among the publicans, and he was rich. [3]And he sought to see Jesus who he was; and could not for the press, because he was little of stature. [4]And he ran before, and climbed up into a sycamore tree to see him: for he was to pass that way. [5]And when Jesus came to the place, he looked up, and saw him, and said unto him, Zaccheus, make haste, and come down; for today I must abide at thy house. [6]And he made haste, and came down, and received him joyfully. [7]And when they saw it, they all murmured, saying, That he was gone to be guest with a man that is a sinner. [8]And Zaccheus stood, and said unto the Lord; Behold, Lord, the half of my goods I give to the poor; and if I have taken any thing from any man by false accusation, I restore him fourfold. [9]And Jesus said unto him, This day is salvation come to this house, forsomuch as he also is a son of Abraham. [10]For the Son of man is come to seek and to save that which was lost.

And, behold, two of them went that same day to a village called Emmaus, which was from Jerusalem about threescore forlongs. And they talked together of all these things which had happened. [15]And it came to pass, that, while they communed together and reasoned, Jesus himself drew near, and went with them. [16]But their eyes were holden that they should not know him. [17]And he said unto them, What manner of communications are these that ye have one to another, as ye talk, and are sad? [18]And the one of them, whose name was Cleopas, answering said unto him, Art thou only a stranger in Jerusalem, and hast not known the things which are come to pass there in these days? [19]And he said unto the, What things? And they said unto him, Concerning Jesus of Nazareth, which was a prophet mighty in deed and word before God and all the people:

[20]And how the chief priests and our rulers delivered him to be condemned to death, and have crucified him. [21]But we trusted that it had been he which should have redeemed Israel: and beside all this, today is the third day since these things were done. [22]Yea, and certain women also of our company made us astonished, which were early at the sepulchre; [23]and when they found not his body, they came, saying, that they had also seen a vision of angels, which said that he was alive. [24]And certain of them which were with us went to the sepulchre, and found it even so as the women had said: but him they saw not. [25]Then he said unto them, O fools, and slow of heart to believe all that the prophets have spoken.

ohn the evangelist, is one of the twelve apostles, traditionally the author of five of the books of the N.T. Like the other evangelists he was portrayed with a quill and a scroll. The evangelist John, and St.John the apostle are believed to have been one and the same person. As member of a Galilean fishing family, he first appears with his brother James and their father Zebedee. Jesus called him and his brothers, who were to become an inner circle around Jesus. As a member of this group, John witnessed some of the most dramatic moments in Jesus' career, e.g.: At the awakening of Jairus' daughter, Jesus did not want anybody accompanying him, but John, Peter and James. At the Transfiguration, only those three were present. At the Mount of Olives those three disciples were especially pointed out by Jesus. At the Last Supper, John leaned back on Jesus' breast and is described as "the disciple, whom Jesus loved". According to tradition passed on by Papias, John later went to Ephesus, was exiled to Patmos and there wrote the Revelation. He returned to Ephesus and composed the Gospel and the Epistles. He reportedly died at a very old age after the turn of the century. His symbol is the Eagle.

nd the third day there was a marriage in Cana of Gallilee; and the mother of Jesus was there: [2]And both Jesus was called, and his disciples, to the marriage. [3]And when they wanted wine, the mother of Jesus saith unto him, They have no wine. [4]Jesus saith unto her, Woman, what have I to do with thee? mine hour is not yet come. [5]His mother saith unto the servants, Whatsoever he saith unto you, do it. [6]And there were set there six waterpots of stone, after the manner of the purifying of the Jews, containing two or three firkins apiece. [7]Jesus saith unto them, Fill the waterpots with water. And they filled them up to the brim. [8]And he saith unto them, Draw out now, and bear unto the governor of the feast. And they bare it. [9]When the ruler of the feast had tasted the water that was made wine, and knew not whence it was, (but the servants which drew the water knew,) the governor of the feast called the bridgroom, [10]And saith unto him, Every man at the beginning doth set forth good wine; and when men have well drunk, then that which is worse: but thou hast kept the good wine until now. [11]This beginning of miracles did Jesus in Cana of Galilee, and manifested forth his glory; and his disciples believed on him.

here was a man of the Pharisees, named Nicodemus, a ruler of the Jews: [2]The same came to Jesus by night, and said unto him, Rabbi, we know that thou art a teacher come from God: for no man can do these miracles that thou doest, except God be with him. [3]Jesus answered and said unto him, Verily, verily, I say unto thee, Except a man be born again, he cannot see the kingdom of God. [4]Nicodemus saith unto him, How can a man be born when he is old? can he enter the second time into his mother's womb, and be born? [5]Jesus answered, Verily, verily, I say unto thee, Except a man be born of water and of the Spirit, he cannot enter into the kingdom of God. [6]That which is born of the flesh is flesh; and that which is born of the Spirit is spirit. [7]Marvel not that I said unto thee, Ye must be born again. [8]The wind bloweth where it listeth, and thou hearest the sound thereof, but canst not tell whence it cometh, and whither it goeth: so is every one that is born of the Spirit. [9]Nicodemus answered and said unto him, How can these things be? [10]Jesus answered and said unto him, Art thou a master of Israel, and knowest not these things? [11]Verily, verily, I say unto thee, We speak that we do know, and testify that we have seen; and ye receive not our witness. [12]If I have told you earthly things, and ye believe not, how shall ye believe, if I tell you of heavenly things? [13]And no man hath ascended up to heaven, but he that came down from heaven, even the Son of man which is in heaven.

nd he must needs go through Samaria. [5]Then cometh he to a city of Samaria, which is called Sychar, near to the parcel of ground that Jacob gave to his son Joseph. [6]Now Jacob's well was there. Jesus therefore, being wearied with his jouney, sat thus on the well: and it was about the sixth hour. [7]There cometh a woman of Samaria to draw water: Jesus saith unto her, Give me to drink. [8](For his disciples were gone away unto the city to buy meat.) [9]Then saith the woman of Samaria unto him, How is it that thou, being a Jew, askest drink of me, which am a woman of Samaria? for the Jews have no dealings with the Samaritans. [10]Jesus answered and said unto her, If thou knewest the gift of God, and who it is that saith to thee, Give me to drink; thou wouldest have asked of him, and he would have given thee living water. [11]The woman saith unto him, Sir, thou hast nothing to draw with, and the well is deep: from whence then hast thou that living water? [12]Art thou greater than our father Jacob, which gave us the well, and drank thereof himself, and his children, and his cattle? [13]Jesus answered and said unto her, Whosoever drinketh of this water shall thirst again: [14]But whosoever drinketh of the water that I shall give him shall never thirst; but the water that I shall give him shall be in him a well of water springing up into everlasting life.

hen he heard that Jesus was come out of Judea into Galilee, he went unto him, and besought him that he would come down, and heal his son: for he was at the point of death. [48]Then said Jesus unto him, Except ye see signs and wonders, ye will not believe. [49]The nobleman saith unto him, Sir, come down ere my child die. [50]Jesus saith unto him, Go thy way; thy son liveth. And the man believed the word that Jesus had spoken unto him, and he went his way. [51]And as he was now going down, his servants met him, and told him, saying, Thy son liveth. [52]Then inquired he of them the hour when he began to amend. And they said unto him, Yesterday at seventh hour the fever left him. [53]So the father knew that it was at the same hour, in the which Jesus said unto him, Thy son liveth: and himself believed, and his whole house. [54]This is again the second miracle that Jesus did, when he was come out of Judea into Galilee.

fter these things Jesus went over the sea of Galilee, which is the sea of Tiberias. [2]And a great multitude followed him, because they saw his miracles which he did on them that were diseased. [3]And Jesus went up into a mountain, and there he sat with his disciples. [4]And the passover, a feast of the Jews, was nigh. [5]When Jesus then lifted up his eyes, and saw a great company come unto him, he saith unto Philip, Whence shall we buy bread, that these may eat? [6]And this he said to prove him: for he himself knew what he would do. [7]Philip answered him, Two hundred pennyworth of bread is not sufficient for them, that every one of them may take a little. [8]One of his disciples, Andrew, Simon Peter's brother, saith unto him, [9]There is a lad here, which hath five barley loaves, and two small fishes: but what are they among so many? [10]And Jesus said, Make the men sit down. Now there was much grass in the place. So the men sat down, in number about five thousand. [11]And Jesus took the loaves; and when he had given thanks, he distributed to the disciples, and the disciples to them that were set down; and likewise of the fishes as much as they would. [12]When they were filled, he said unto his disciples, Gather up the fragments that remain, that nothing be lost. [13]Therefore they gathered them together, and filled twelve baskets with the fragments of the five barley loaves, which remained over and above unto them that had eaten. [14]Then those men, when they had seen the miracle that Jesus did, said, This is of a truth that prophet that should come into the world. [15]When Jesus therefore perceived that they would come and take him by force, to make him a king, he departed again into a mountain himself alone.

esus went unto the mount of Olives. ²And early in the morning he came again into the temple, and all the people came unto him; and he sat down, and taught them. ³And the scribes and Pharisees brought unto him a woman taken in adultery; and when they had set her in the midst, ⁴They say unto him, Master, this woman was taken in adultery, in the very act. ⁵Now Moses in the law commanded us, that such should be stoned: but what sayest thou? ⁶This they said, tempting him, that they might have to accuse him. But Jesus stooped down, and with his finger wrote on the ground, as though he heard them not. ⁷So when they continued asking him, he lifted up himself, and said unto them, He that is without sin among you, let him first cast a stone at her. ⁸And again he stooped down, and wrote on the ground. ⁹And they which heard it, being convicted by their own conscience, went out one by one, beginning at the eldest, even unto the last: and Jesus was left alone, and the woman standing in the midst. ¹⁰When Jesus had lifted up himself, and saw none but the woman, he said unto her, Woman, where are those thine accusers? hath no man condemned thee? ¹¹She said, No man, Lord. And Jesus said unto her, Neither do I condemn thee: go, and sin no more.

hen when Mary was come where Jesus was, and saw him, she fell down at his feet, saying unto him, Lord, if thou hadst been here, my brother had not died. [33]When Jesus therefore saw her weeping, and the Jews also weeping which came with her, he groaned in the spirit, and was troubled, [34]And said, Where have ye laid him? They said unto him, Lord, come and see. [35]Jesus wept. [36]Then said the Jews, Behold how he loved him! [37]And some of them said, Could not this man, which opened the eyes of the blind, have caused that even this man should not have died? [38]Jesus therefore again groaning in himself cometh to the grave. It was a cave, and a stone lay upon it. [39]Jesus said, Take ye away the stone. Martha, the sister of him, that was dead, saith unto him, Lord, by this time he stinketh: for he hath been dead four days. [40]Jesus saith unto her, Said I not unto thee, that, if thou wouldest believe, thou shouldest see the glory of God? [41]Then they took away the stone from the place where the dead was laid. And Jesus lifted up his eyes, and said, Father, I thank thee that thou hast heard me. [42]And I knew that thou hearest me always: but because of the people which stand by I said it, that they may believe that thou hast sent me. [43]And when he thus had spoken, he cried with a loud voice, Lazarus, come forth. [44]And he that was dead came forth, bound hand and foot with graveclothes: and his face was bound about with a napkin. Jesus saith unto them, Loose him, and let him go. [45]Then many of the Jews which came to Mary, and had seen the things which Jesus did, believed on him.

hen came Jesus forth, wearing the crown of thorns, and the purple robe. And Pilate saith unto them, Behold the man! [6]When the chief priests therefore and officers saw him, they cried out, saying, Crucify him, crucify him. Pilate saith unto them, Take ye him, and crucify him: for I find no fault in him. [7]The Jews answered him, We have a law, and by our law he ought to die, because he made himself the Son of God. [8]When Pilate therefore heard that saying, he was the more afraid; [9]And went again into the judgment hall, and saith unto Jesus, Whence art thou? But Jesus gave him no answer. [10]Then saith Pilate unto him, Speakest thou not unto me? knowest thou not that I have power to crucify thee, and have power to release thee? [11]Jesus answered, Thou couldest have no power at all against me, except it were given thee from above: therefore he that delivered me unto thee hath the greater sin. [12]And from thenceforth Pilate sought to release him: but the Jews cried out, saying, If thou let this man go, thou art not Cesar's friend: whosoever maketh himself a king speak-eth against Cesar. [13]When Pilate therefore heard that saying, he brought Jesus forth, and sat down in the judgment seat in a place that is called the Pavement, but in the Hebrew, Gabbatha. [14]And it was the preparation of the passover, and about the sixth hour: and he saith unto the Jews, Behold your King! [15]But they cried out, Away with him, away with him, crucify him. Pilate saith unto them, Shall I crucify your King? The chief priests answered, We have no king but Cesar. [16]Then delivered he him therefore unto them to be crucified. And they took Jesus, and led him away.

hen they therefore were come together, they asked of him, saying, Lord, wilt thou at this time restore again the kingdom to Israel? [7]And he said unto them, It is not for you to know the times or the seasons, which the Father hath put in his own power. [8]But ye shall receive power, after that the Holy Ghost is come upon you: and ye shall be witnesses unto me both in Jerusalem, and in all Judea, and in Samaria, and unto the uttermost part of the earth. [9]And when he had spoken these things, while they beheld, he was taken up; and a cloud received him out of their sight. [10]And while they looked stedfastly toward heaven as he went up, behold, two men stood by them in white apparel; [11]Which also said, Ye men of Galilee, why stand ye gazing up into heaven? this same Jesus, which is taken up from you into heaven, shall so come in like manner as ye have seen him go into heaven.

nd there appeared unto them cloven tongues like as of fire, and it sat upon each of them. [4]And they were all filled with the Holy Ghost, and began to speak with other tongues, as the Spirit gave them utterance. [5]And there were dwelling at Jerusalem Jews, devout men, out of every nation under heaven. [6]Now when this was noised abroad, the multitude came together, and were confounded, because that every man heard them speak in his own language. [7]And they were all amazed and marvelled, saying one to another, Behold, are not all these which speak Galileans? [8]And how hear we every man in our own tongue, wherein we were born? [9]Parthians, and Medes, and Elamites, and the dwellers in Mesopotamia, and in Judea, and Cappadocia, in Pontus, and Asia, [10]Phrygia, and Pamhpylia, in Egypt, and in the parts of Libya about Carene, and strangers of Rome, Jews and proselytes, [11]Cretes and Arabians, we do hear them speak in our tongues the wonderful works of God. [12]And they were all amazed, and were in doubt, saying one to another, What meaneth this? [13]Others mocking said, These men are full of new wine. [14]But Peter, standing up with the eleven, lifted up his voice, and said unto them, Ye men of Judea, and all ye that dwell at Jerusalem, be this known unto you, and hearken to my words: [15]or these are not drunken, as ye suppose, seeing it is but the third hour of the day. [16]But this is that which was spoken by the prophet Joel;

ow Peter and John went up together into the temple at the hour of prayer, being the ninth hour. [2]And a certain man lame from his mother's womb was carried, whom they laid daily at the gate of the temple which is called Beautiful, to ask alms of them that entered into the temple; [3]Who seeing Peter and John about to go into the temple asked an alms. [4]And Peter, fastening his eyes upon him with John, said, Look on us. [5]And he gave heed unto them, expecting to receive something of them. [6]Then Peter said, Silver and gold have I none; but such as I have give I thee: In the name of Jesus Christ of Nazareth rise up and walk. [7]And he took him by the right hand, and lifted him up: and immediately his feet and ankle bones received strength. [8]And he leaping up stood, and walked, and entered with them into the temple, walking, and leaping, and praising God. [9]And all the people saw him walking and praising God: [10]And they knew that it was he which sat for alms at the Beautiful gate of the temple: and they were filled with wonder and amazement at that which had happened unto him. [11]And as the lame man which was healed held Peter and John, all the people ran together unto them in the porch that is called Solomon's greatly wondering.

ut a certain man named Ananias, with Sapphira his wife, sold a possession, [2]And kept back part of the price, his wife also being privy to it, and brought a certain part, and laid it at the apostles' feet. [3]But Peter said, Ananias, why hath Satan filled thine heart to lie to the Holy Ghost, and to keep back part of the price of the land? [4]While it remained, was it not thine own? and after it was sold, was it not in thine own power? why hast thou conceived this thing in thine heart? thou hast not lied unto men, but unto God. [5]And Ananias hearing these words fell down, and gave up the ghost: and great fear came on all them that heard these things. [6]And the young men arose, wound him up, and carried him out, and buried him. [7]And it was about the space of three hours after, when his wife, not knowing what was done, came in. [8]And Peter answered unto her, Tell me whether ye sold the land for so much? And she said, Yea, for so much. [9]Then Peter said unto her, How is it that ye have agreed together to tempt the Spirit of the Lord? behold, the feet of them which have buried thy husband are at the door, and shall carry thee out. [10]Then fell she down straightwar at his feet, and yielded up the ghost: and the young men came in, and found her dead, and, carrying her forth, buried her by her husband. [11]And great fear came upon all the church, and upon as many as heard these things.

231

hen they heard these things, they were cut to the heart, and they gnashed on him with their teeth. [55]But he, being full of the Holy Ghost, looked up steadfastly into heaven, and saw the glory of God, and Jesus standing on the right hand of God. [56]And said, Behold, I see the heavens opened, and the Son of man standing on the right hand of God. [57]Then they cried out with a loud voice, and stopped their ears, and ran upon him with one accord, [58]And cast him out of the city, and stoned him: and the witnesses laid down their clothes at a young man's feet, whose name was Saul. [59]And they stoned Stephen, calling upon God, and saying, Lord Jesus, receive my spirit. [60]And he kneeled down, and cried with a loud voice, Lord, lay not this sin to their charge. And when he had said this, he fell asleep.

nd as they went on their way, they came unto a certain water: and the eunuch said, See, here is water; what doth hinder me to be baptized? [37]And Philip said, If thou believest with all thine heart, thou mayest. And he answered and said, I believe that Jesus Christ is the Son of God. [38]And he commanded the chariot to stand still: and they went down both into the water, both Philip and the eunuch; and he baptized him. [39]And when they were come up out of the water, the Spirit of the Lord caught away Philip, that the eunuch saw him no more: and he went on his way rejoicing. [40]But Philip was found at Azotus: and passing through he preached in all the cities, till he came to Cesarea.

nd Saul, yet breathing out threatnings and slaughter against the disciples of the Lord, went unto the high priest, [2]And desired of him letters to Damascus to the synagogues, that if he found any of this way, whether they were men or women, he might bring them bound unto Jerusalem. [3]And as he journeyed, he came near Damascus: and suddenly there shined round about him a light from heaven: [4]And he fell to the earth, and heard a voice saying unto him, Saul, Saul, why persecutest thou me? [5]And he said, Who art thou, Lord? And the Lord said, I am Jesus whom thou persecutest: it is hard for thee to kick against the pricks. [6]And he trembling and astonished said, Lord, what wilt thou have me to do? And the Lord said unto him, Arise, and go into the city, and it shall be told thee what thou must do. [7]And the men which journeyed with him stood speechless, hearing a voice, but seeing no man. [8]And Saul arose from the earth; and when his eyes were opened, he saw no man: but they led him by the hand, and brought him into Damascus. [9]And he was three days without sight, and neither did eat nor drink. [10]And there was a certain disciple at Damascus, named Ananias; and to him said the Lord in a vision, Ananias. And he said, Behold, I am here, Lord. [11]And the Lord said unto him, Arise, and go into the street which is called Straight, and inquire in the house of Judas for one called Saul, of Tarsus: for, behold, he prayeth, [12]And hath seen in a vision a man named Ananias coming in, and putting his hand on mine, that he might receive his sight.

here was a certain man in Cesarea called Cornelius, a centurion of the band called the Italian band, [2]A devout man, and one that feared God with all his house, which gave much alms to the people, and prayed to God alway. [3]He saw in a vision evidently about the ninth hour of the day an angel of God coming in to him, and saying unto him, Cornelius. [4]And when he looked on him, he was afraid, and said, What is it, Lord? And he said unto him, Thy prayers and thine alms are come up for a memorial before God. [5]And now send men to Joppa, and call for one Simon, Whose surname is Peter: [6]He lodgeth with one Simon a tanner, whose house is by the sea side: he shall tell thee what thou oughtest to do. [7]And when the angel which spake unto Cornelius was departed, he called two of his household servants, and a devout soldier of them that waited on him continually; [8]And when he had declared all these things unto them, he sent them to Joppa. [9]On the morrow, as they went on their journey, and drew nigh unto the city, Peter went up upon the housetop to pray about the sixth hour: [10]And he became very hungry, and would have eaten: but while they made ready, he fell into a trance, [11]And saw heaven opened, and a certain vessel descending unto him, as it had been a great sheet knit at the four corners, and let down to the earth: [12]Wherein were all manner of fourfooted beasts of the earth, and wild beasts, and creeping things, and fowls of the air. [13]And there came a voice to him, Rise, Peter; kill, and eat. [14]But Peter said, Not so, Lord; for I have never eaten any thing that is common or unclean. [15]And the voice spake unto him again the second time, What God hath cleansed, that call not thou common. [16]This was done thrice: and the vessel was received up again into heaven.

Now about that time Herod the king stretched forth his hands to vex certain of the church. ²And he killed James the brother of John with the sword. ³And because he saw it pleased the Jews, he proceeded further to take Peter also. (Then were the days of unleavened bread.) ⁴And when he had apprehendend him, he put him in prison, and delivered him to four quaternions of soldiers to keep him; intending after Easter to bring him forth to the people. ⁵Peter therefore was kept in prison: but prayer was made without ceasing of the church unto God for him. ⁶And when Herod would have brought him forth, the same night Peter was sleeping between two soldiers, bound with two chains: and the keepers before the door kept the prison. ⁷And, behold, the angel of the Lord came upon him, and a light shined in the prison: and he smote Peter on the side, and raised him up, saying, Arise up quickly. And his chains fell off from his hands. ⁸And the angel said unto him, Gird thyself, and bind on thy sandals. And so he did. And he saith unto him, Cast thy garment about thee, and follow me. ⁹And he went out, and followed him; and wist not that it was true which was done by the angel; but thought he saw a vision. ¹⁰When they were past the first and the second ward, they came unto the iron gate that leadeth unto the city; which opened to them of his own accord: and they went out, and passed on through one street; and forthwith the angel departed from him. ¹¹And when Peter was come to himself, he said, Now I know of asurety, that the Lord hath sent his angel, and hath delivered me out of the hand of Herod, and from all the expectation of the people of the Jews.

nd there sat a certain man at Lystra, impotent in his feet, being a cripple from his mother's womb, who never had walked: [9]The same heard Paul speak: who steadfastly beholding him, and perceiving that he had faith to be healed, [10]Said with a loud voice, Stand upright on thy feet. And he leaped and walked. [11]And when the people saw what Paul had done, they lifted up their voices, saying in the speech of Lycaonia, The gods are come down to us in the likeness of men. [12]And they called Barnabas, Jupiter; and Paul, Mercurius, because he was the chief speaker.

nd when they had ta-
ken up the anchors,
they committed them-
selves unto the sea, and
loosed the rudder
bands, and hoisted up
the mainsail to the
wind, and made toward shore. [41]And falling
into a place where two seas met, they ran
the ship aground; and the forepart stuck fast,
and remained unmoveable, but the hinder
part was broken with the violence of the
waves. [42]And the soldiers counsel was to kill
the prisoners, lest any of them should swim
out, and escape. [43]But the centurion, willing to
save Paul, kept them from their purpose; and
commanded that they which could swim
should cast themselves first into the sea, and
get to land: [44]And the rest, some on boards,
and some on broken pieces of the ship. And
so it came to pass, that they escaped all safe
to land.

 was in the Spirit on the Lord's day, and heard behind me a great voice, as of a trumpet, [11]Saying, I am Alpha and Omega, the first and the last: and, What thou seest, write in a book, and send it unto the seven churches which are in Asia; unto Ephesus, and unto Smyrna, and unto Pergamos, and unto Thyatira, and unto Sardis, and unto Philadelphia, and unto Laodicea. [12]And I turned to see the voice that spake with me. And being turned, I saw seven golden candlesticks; [13]And in the midst of the seven candlesticks one like unto the Son of man, clothed with a garment down to the foot, and girt about the paps with a golden girdle. [14]His head and his hairs were white like wool, as white as snow; and his eyes were as a flame of fire; [15]And his feet like unto fine brass, as if they burned in a furnace; and his voice as the sound of many waters. [16]And he had in his right hand seven stars: and out of his mouth went a sharp two-edged sword: and his countenance was as the sun shineth in his strength. [17]And when I saw him, I fell at his feet as dead. And he laid his right hand upon me, saying unto me, Fear not; I am the first and the last: [18]I am he that liveth, and was dead; and, behold, I am alive for evermore, Amen; and have the keys of hell and of death. [19]Write the things which thou hast seen, and the things which are, and the things which shall be hereafter; [20]The mystery of the seven stars which thou sawest in my right hand, and the seven golden candlesticks. The seven stars are the angels of the seven churches: and the seven candlesticks which thou sawest are the seven churches.

nd immediately I was in the spirit; and, behold, a throne was set in heaven, and one sat on the throne. ³And he that sat was to look upon like a jaspar and a sardine stone: and there was a rainbow round about the throne, in sight like unto an emerald. ⁴And round about the throne were four and twenty seats: and upon the seats I saw four and twenty elders sitting, clothed in white raiment; and they had on their heads crowns of gold. ⁵And out of the throne proceeded lightnings and thunderings and voices: and there were seven lamps of fire burning before the throne, which are the seven Spirits of God. ⁶And before the throne there was a sea of glass like unto crystal: and in the midst of the throne, and round about the throne, were four beasts full of eyes before and behind. ⁷And the first beast was like a lion, and the second beast like a calf, and the third beast had a face as a man,

and the fourth beast was like a flying eagle. ⁸And the four beasts had each of them six wings about him; and they were full of eyes within: and they rest not day and night, saying, Holy, holy, holy, Lᴏʀᴅ God Almighty, which was, and is, and is to come.

nd I saw, and behold a white horse: and he that sat on him had a bow; and a crown was given unto him: and he went forth conquering, and to conquer. ³And when he had opened the second seal, I heard the second beast say, Come and see. ⁴And there went out another horse that was red: and power was given to him that sat thereon to take peace from the earth, and that they should kill one another: and there was given unto him a great sword. ⁵And when he had opened the third seal, I heard the third beast say, Come and see. And I beheld, and lo a black horse; and he that sat on him had a pair of balances in his hand. ⁶And I heard a voice in the midst of the four beasts say, A measure of wheat for a penny, and three measures of barley for a penny; and see thou hurt not the oil and the wine. ⁷And when he had opened the fourth seal, I heard the voice of the fourth beast say, Come and see. ⁸And I looked, and behold a pale horse: and his name that sat on him was Death, and Hell followed with him. And power was given unto them over the fourth part of the earth, to kill with sword, and with hunger, and with death, and with the beasts of the earth. ⁹And when he had opened the fifth seal, I saw under the altar the souls of them that were slain for the word of God, and for the testimony which they held: ¹⁰And they cried with a loud voice, saying, How long, O Lord, holy and true, dost thou not judge and avenge our blood on them that dwell on the earth? ¹¹And white robes were given unto every one of them; and it was said unto them, that they should rest yet for a little season, until their fellow-servants also and their brethren, that should be killed as they were, would be fulfilled. ¹²And I beheld when he had opened the sixth seal, and, lo, there was a great earthquake; and the sun became black as sackcloth of hair, and the moon became as blood;

nd the seven angels which had the seven trumpets prepared themselves to sound. [7]The first angel sounded, and here followed hail and fire mingled with blood, and they were cast upon the earth: and the third part of trees was burnt up, and all green grass was burnt up. [8]And the second angel sounded, and as it were a great mountain burning with fire was cast into the sea: and the third part of the sea became blood; [9]And the third part of the creatures which were in the sea, and had life, died; and the third part of the ships were destroyed. [10]And the third angel sounded, and there fell a great star from heaven, burning as it were a lamp, and it fell upon the third part of the rivers, and upon the fountains of waters; [11]And the name of the star is called Wormwood; and the third part of the waters became wormwood; and many died of the waters, because they were made bitter.

[12]And the fourth angel sounded, and the third part of the sun was smitten, and the third part of the moon, and the third part of the stars; so as the third part of them was darkened, and the day shone not for a third part of it, and the night likewise.

nd the shapes of the locusts were like upon horses prepared unto battle; and on their heads were as it were crowns like gold, and their faces were as the faces of men. [8]And they had hair as the hair of women, and their teeth were as the teeth of lions. [9]And they had breastplates, as it were breastplates of iron; and the sound of their wings was as the sound of chariots of many horses running to battle. [10]And they had tails like unto scorpions, and there were stings in their tails: and their power was a hurt men five months. [11]And they had a king over them, which is the angel of the bottomless pit, whose name in the Hebrew tongue is Abaddon, but in the Greek tongue hath his name Apollyon. [12]One woe is past; and, behold, there come two woes more hereafter. [13]And the sixth angel sounded, and I heard a voice from the four horns of the golden altar which is before God,

[14]Saying to the sixth angel which hand the trumpet, Loose the four angels which are bound in the great river Euphrates. [15]And the four angels were loosed, which were prepared for an hour, and a day, and a month, and a year, for to slay the third part of men. [16]And the number of the army of the horsemen were two hundred thousand thousand: and I heard the number of them. [17]And thus I saw the horses in the vision, and them that sat on them, having breastplates of fire, and of jacinth, and brimstone: and the heads of the horses were as the heads of lions: and out of their mouths issued fire and smoke and brimstone. [18]By these three was the third part of men killed, by the fire, and by the smoke, and by the brimstone, which issued out of their mouths.

nd I saw another mighty angel come down from heaven, clothed with a cloud: and a rainbow was upon his head, and his face was as it were the sun, and his feet as pillars of fire: [2]And he had in his hand a little book open: and he set his right foot upon the sea, and his left foot on the earth, [3]And cried with a loud voice, as when a lion roareth: and when he had cried, seven thunders uttered their voices. [4]And when the seven thunders had uttered their voices, I was about to write: and I heard a voice from heaven saying unto me, Seal up those things which the seven thunders uttered, and write them not. [5]And the angel which I saw stand upon the sea and upon the earth lifted up his hand to heaven, [6]And sware by him that liveth for ever and ever, who created heaven, and the things that therein are, and the earth, and the things that therein are, and the sea, and the things which are therein, that there should be time no longer: [7]But in the days of the voice of the seventh angel, when he shall begin to sound, the mystery of God should be finished, as he hath declared to his servants the prophets.

And when they shall have finished their testimony, the beast that ascendeth out of the bottomless pit shall make war against them, and shall overcome them, and kill them. ⁸And their dead bodies shall lie in the street of the great city, which spiritually is called Sodom and Egypt, where also our Lord was crucified. ⁹And they of the people and kindreds and tongues and nations shall see their dead bodies three days and half, and shall not suffer their dead bodies to be put in graves. ¹⁰And they that dwell upon the earth shall rejoice over them, and make merry, and shall send gifts one to another; because these two prophets tormented them that dwelt on the earth. ¹¹And after three days and an half the Spirit of life from God entered into them, and they stood upon their feet; and great fear fell upon them which saw them. ¹²And they heard a great voice from heaven saying unto them, Come up hither. And they ascended up to heaven in a cloud; and their enemies beheld them. ¹³And the same hour was there a great earthquake, and the tenth part of the city fell, and in the earthquake were slain of men seven thousand: and the remnant were affrighted, and gave glory to the God of heaven. ¹⁴The second woe is past; and, behold, the third woe cometh quickly.

nd I stood upon the sand of the sea, and saw a beast rise up out of the sea, having seven heads and ten horns, and upon his horns ten crowns, and upon his heads the name of blasphemy. [2]And the beast which I saw was like unto a leopard, and his feet were as the feet of a bear, and his mouth as the mouth of a lion: and the dragon gave him his power, and his seat, and great authority. [3]And I saw one of his heads as it were wounded to death; and his deadly wound was healed: and all the world wondered after the beast. [4]And they worshipped the dragon which gave power unto the beast: and they worshipped the beast, saying, Who is like unto the beast? who is able to make war with him? [5]And there was given unto him a mouth speaking great things and blasphemies; and power was given unto him to continue forty and two months. [6]And he opened his mouth in blasphemy against God, to blaspheme his name, and his tabernacle, and them that dwell in heaven.

nd I heard a great voice out of the temple saying to the seven angels, Go your ways, and pour out the vials of the wrath of God upon the earth. nd the sixth angel poured out his vital upon the great river Euphrates, and the water thereof was dried up, that the way of the kings of the east might be prepared. [13]And I saw three unclean spirits like frogs come out of the mouth of the dragon, and out of the mouth of the beast, and out of the mouth of the false prophet. [14]For they are the spirits of devils, working miracles, which go forth unto the kings of the earth and of the whole world, to gather them to the battle of that great day of God Almighty. [15]Behold, I come as a thief. Blessed is he that watchesth, and keepeth his garments, lest he walk naked, and they see his shame. [16]And he gathered them together into a place called in the Hebrew tongue Armageddon.

or in one hour so great riches is come to nought. And every shipmaster, and all the company in ships, and sailors, and as many as trade by sea, stood afar off, [18]And cried when they saw the smoke of her burning, saying, What city is like unto this great city! [19]And they cast dust on their heads, and cried, weeping and wailing, saying, Alas, alas, that great city, wherein were made rich all that had ships in the sea by reason of her costliness! for in one hour is she made desolate. [20]Rejoice over her, thou heaven, and ye holy apostles and prophets; for God hath avenged you on her. [21]And a mighty angel took up a stone like a great millstone, and cast it into the sea, saying, Thus with violence shall that great city Babylon be thrown down, and shall be found no more at all. [22]And the voice of harpers, and musicians, and of pipers, and trumpeters, shall be heard no more at all in thee; and no craftsman, of whatsoever craft he be, shall be found any more in thee; and the sound of a millstone shall be heard no more at all in thee; [23]And the light of a candle shall shine no more at all in thee; and the voice of the bridegroom and of the bride shall be heard no more at all in thee: for thy merchants were the great men of the earth; for by thy sorceries were all nations deceived. [24]And in her was found the blood of prophets, and of saints, and of all that were slain upon the earth.

And I saw an angel come down form heaven, having the key of the bottomless pit and a great chain in his hand. [2]And he laid hold on the dragon, that old serpent, which is the Devil, and Satan, and bound him a thousand years, [3]And cast him into the bottomless pit, and shut him up, and set a seal upon him, that he should deceive the nations no more, till the thousand years should be fulfilled: and after that he must be loosed a little season. [4]And I saw thrones, and they sat upon them, and judgment was given unto them: and I saw the souls of them that were beheaded for the witness of Jesus, and for the word of God, and which had not worshipped the beast, neither his image, neither had received his mark upon their foreheads, or in their hands; and they lived and reigned with Christ a thousand years. [5]But the rest of the dead lived not again until the thousand years were finished. This is the first resurrection. [6]Blessed and holy is he that hath part in the first resurrection: on such the second death hath no power, but they shall be priests of God and of Christ, and shall reign with him a thousand years. [7]And when the thousand years are expired, Satan shall be loosed out of his prison, [8]And shall go out to deceive the nations which are in the four quarters of the earth, Gog and Magog, to gather them together to battle: the number of whom is as the sand of the sea. [9]And they went up on the breadth of the earth, and compassed the camp of the saints about, and the beloved city: and fire came down from God out of heaven, and devoured them.

nd he cried me away in the spirit to a great and high mountain, and shewed me that great city, the holy Jerusalem, descending out of heaven from God, [11]Having the glory of God: and her light was like unto a stone most precious, even like a jasper stone, clear as crystal; [12]And had a wall great and high, and had twelve gates, and at the gates twelve angels, and names written thereon, which are the names of the twelve tribes of the children of Israel: [13]On the east three gates; on the north three gates; on the south three gates; and on the west three gates. [14]And the wall of the city had twelve foundations, and in them the names of the twelve apostles of the Lamb. [15]And he that talked with me had a golden reed to measure the city, and the gates thereof, and the wall thereof. [16]And the city lieth foursquare, and the length is as large as the breadth: and he measured the city with the reed, twelve thousand furlongs. The length and the breadth and the height of it are equal. [17]And he measured the wall thereof, and hundred and forty and four cubits, according to the measure of a man, that is, of the angel. [18]And the building of the wall of it was of jasper: and the city was pure gold, like unto clear glass. [19]And the foundations of the wall of the city were garnished with all manner of precious stones. The first foundation was jasper; the second, sapphire; the third, a chalcedony; the fourth an emerald; [20]The fifth, sardonyx: the sixth, sardius; the seventh, chrysolyte; the eighth, beryl; the ninth, a topaz; the tenth, a chrysoprasus; the eleventh, a jacinth; the twelfth, an amethyst. [21]And the twelve gates were twelve pearls: every several gate was of one pearl: and the street of the city was pure gold, as it were transparent glass.

Index

The Old Testament